Powerful
Steps

10 Essential Career Skills and Business Strategies for the Workplace Warrior

Foreword By *Wally "Famous" Amos*

Brian J. Bieler

Published By:
Little Falls Press
7000 North 16th Street, Suite 120 # 489
Phoenix, AZ 85020-5547

powerfulsteps@cox.net

Visit our website at http://www.powerfulsteps.com

Unattributed quotations are by Brian J. Bieler

Powerful Steps:
10 Essential Career Skills
and Business Strategies
for the Workplace Warrior

ISBN-13: 978-0-9779569-1-3
ISBN-10: 0-9779569-1-1

Cover design by Blue Bus Media
Los Angeles, CA 310-985-5165
www.bluebusmedia.com

Acknowledgements

To my wife Ann, always by my side and my best supporter who put up with our moves all over the country. To my children Jeff, Drew and Danielle thank you for your love and support. To my daughter-in law Lisa, my grandson Cameron, my brother Allan and my uncle Jerry "Jeep" Bieler who helped me get started.

And many thanks to those who helped me along the way, Sid Levine, Howie Jacobs, Mark Forster, Marvin Tinsley, Thom Winters, Ellyn Ambrose, Steve Martin, Norman Feuer, Hal Gore, Woody Sudbrink, Bill McEntee, Omnis Aceabo, Kathy Seip, Linda Scott, Peter Fulton, Peter Irmiter, Joyce Beber, Elaine Silverstein, Julio Rumbaut, Bud Saltzman, Marty Cohen, Dave Baiata, Mary Savoy, George Toulas, Kent Burkhart, Rand Gottleib, Rick Seaby, Mike Vince, Richard A. Forman, Niles Seaburg, David Saperstein, Shane Coppola, Jim Shulke, Jerry Del Colliano, John Furman, Stan Mouse, Bob Duffy, Bill Fortenbaugh, Charlie Columbo, Bruce Blevins, Mike Brandt, David Sousa, Harvy Tate, Steve Crumbly, Brock Whaley, Debbie Calton, Tom Birch, Courtney Thompson, T. J. Malievsky, Hutch Huthinson, Andy Worden, Lee "Baby" Sims, Robert "Rabbett" Abbet, "Mr. Bill" Mims, Don Mueller, Dick Casper, Lan Roberts, Andy Preston, Andy Worden, Mike Evans, Mike Vasser, Don Mueller, Earl McDaniel, Ken Rosene, Stewart Shapiro, Jeff Coelho, Ed Gargano, Joe Davidman, Kevin Beacraft, Frank Byrne, Debbie White, Paul Hughes, Bob Cole, Jim London, E. Karl, Terry Wood, Venita Jameson, Mike Keslo, Terry Elks, Ed Shore, George Wolfson,

Dan Diloreto, Bill Figenshu, Doug Harville, Mike "Murph" Murphy, Larry Lemanski, Mike McVay, Bob Hughes, Jonathan Schwartz, Nick Trigony, Jim Keating, Charles Warner, D. Garry Munson, Bob Harper, Curt Hahn, "Banana" Joe Montione, DC Cordova, Blair Singer, Wayne Morgan, Dale Richardson, Carol Dysart, Michael Head, Dennis Cooney, Peter Meisen, Ashley Gardner, Betty Pearce, Keith J. Cunningham, Peter Johnston and Suzi Dafnis, Dolf de Roos, Bob Burch, Cordy Overgarrd, Shawn Holly, Mark Waters, Dawn Surber, Thom King, Gary Blau, Jim Taszarke, Bruce Olson, Tom Peake, Shawn Holly, Charlie Sislen, Terry Patrick, Jason Kane, Reid Reker, Bob Gad, Bennett Zier, Steve Goldstein, Mick Anselmo, Tom Mooney, Steven Rales, Joe Bunting, Ron Cohen, Matt Hanlon, Darrel Goodin, Jimmy DeCastro, John Coulter, David Lebow, Brian Ongaro, Brenda Adriance, Joel Salkawitz, Pat McMahon, Matt Kisselstein, Michael Nasser, Brian Stone, Jeff Holden, Ken Kohl, Rob Laing, Diane Dubose, Bob Benderson, Mayra DeAnda, Diane Nawrocki, Harv T. Eker, Joey Gilbert, Mark Victor Hansen, Wally "Famous" Amos, Robert and Kim Kiyosaki.

The friend that is nice to you but not nice to the waiter is not your friend.

—Paul Bieler

This book is dedicated to my dad.

Table of Contents

Authors Note: *Wally represents the values and ideals I have put in my book and he is truly one of the most unusual people I have ever met. He is a testimony to all of us that life is never over until we say it is. From a supply clerk at Saks Fifth Avenue to international fame, Wally is a living testimony to "average people" that life is ours for the asking if only we have a positive attitude and dare to take the initiative!*

Foreword
By Wally Amos

My experiences have taught me to shape my own life by changing my attitude about the world I live in. For years, I didn't know what I wanted to do with myself. I only knew what I did not want to do, how I did not want to do it, where I did not want to do it, and who I did not want to do it with. Living my life from such a negative perspective obviously produced negative results. I was not happy at home, when I was there, which wasn't often, and when away I constantly searched, and in all the wrong places, for my life's missing ingredients. I finally found what I had been looking for all those years. The answer lay inside me all along: a change of attitude. A positive attitude tells you that life is never really what it appears to be — it is always more. I changed my attitude and I changed my life.

I was the first black agent at the William Morris Talent Agency in Los Angeles. I was very young but with a great attitude, hard work and enthusiasm worked my way up from the mailroom and being a secretary to representing Marvin Gaye, Diana Ross and the Supremes, Dionne Warwick, Sam Cooke and signed the unknown Simon and Garfunkel to the agency. My success gave me self-esteem and a wonderful entrepreneurial spirit. My Aunt Della gave me a love of chocolate chip cookies. Years later I give away those homemade bite-sized cookies as calling cards during meetings held for my clients. The cookies were so good I was urged to start a cookie business. I thought to myself how many times in our lives have we heard, "You have a great idea, you should do something with it" only to let a dream fade away. I decided I didn't want to be one of those who just talked about something and with the help of my friends Helen Reddy and Marvin Gaye got the start up funds for my new cookie venture.

I used what I learned in show business to market the cookies. In 1975, I launched the Famous Amos Cookie Company and the gourmet cookie industry began. I became the company showman and gave cookies away everywhere I went. I wore a Panama straw hat and bright Hawaiian shirt and put that picture of myself on the bags of cookies. My business went from a cookie store front on Sunset Boulevard in Hollywood to a $10 million dollar business and my hat and shirt was placed in a collection at the Smithsonian Museum of Business Americana in Washington D.C. President Ronald Reagan awarded me the Entrepreneurial Excellence Award in appreciation of an American success story.

In 1989, I lost the business and Famous Amos sued me over ownership of my name and likeness. I had to start out all over again. I started a new company in 1996, Uncle Noname, selling muffins and begin giving lectures on overcoming adversity with a positive attitude.

I have shared a brief portion of my career to show you that life has surprises in store for all of us. The secret to success is not what happens to us. Our success in life is how we *react* to what happens to us. Success in life is rarely a straight line going up. It's filled with wins and disappointments. It's our inner strength and attitude that picks us up after we fall down. Our self–esteem is our strongest asset and keeps us going against the head winds of life.

I met Brian at 98Rock in Honolulu with my cookie calling cards and have followed his outstanding career from general manager to president of Viacom Radio in New York City. He called me when he first started to write Powerful Steps and told me about his idea. Brian said that many people in jobs and careers would never reach their goals and dreams because they focused on the wrong skills. He said so many people have the desire to be successful but just don't understand the secrets of what it takes. In all his years of experience, he saw that success was going to the people that had qualities many ignore or take for granted. Almost all of the enormously successful people he worked with and personally knew were just average people like you and me.

What was different about the successful ones was they had a never-ending sense of value, high self-esteem and a winning positive attitude. Brian saw people succeed not because of education or a high intelligence but because they had mastered communication skills and were clear thinkers. They focused on a willingness to go for it and take action. The successful were more afraid of not succeeding and less worried about failure and risk.

As I look at my successes, I agree with Brian and have learned that attitude is everything and I am in complete control of my attitude. However, attitude alone will only take you so far. You must take action and put your energy and enthusiasm to work or nothing will ever come of your ideas. Thinking about action and taking actions are what separate the average from the successful.

I worked hard at selling cookies and I loved the business. But the real success was my willingness to put myself on the line. People saw my enthusiasm and commitment and that made all the difference

Powerful Steps has important lessons on skills that separate the average from the successful. The skills of leaders, politicians, CEO's and winners are all in his book and any one of them can change your life. How well we develop relationships, how our confidence and communication skills influence others, how to truly understand what others are saying, the importance of being passionate for what we do and how we think and plan our steps. Brian has an insider's view from years of experience working with some of the brightest strategic thinkers who knew how to put fast track strategies to work.

Brian doesn't say success comes easy. He points out that taking the initiative to master the personal skills we are all aware of may be far more important to success in our chosen career than our day to day job or technical skills.

My hope is you will get as much out of this book as I have. It's written in easy to understand language from a master of sales, communication, negotiating and marketing who has made millions for companies and helped average people reach their potential.

Here's to you being the best you can be and remember all success starts with your attitude. I hope you enjoy what you discover in this book and be sure to read it to the end. The stories and ideas may surprise you how truly great things can happen when ordinary people are focused and determined to become winners. The material in *Powerful Steps* to success absolutely work, *if you work them.*

Wally Amos, Author, *Be Positive, Be Positive!*
www.wallyamos.com

Introduction

The failure is not to participate.

The majority of successful people have personal skills exceeding natural talent or education. Exceptions are professionals, athletes, movie stars and those with extraordinary abilities. These people enjoy huge incomes and success regardless of other skills. For the rest of us who put our pants on one leg at a time, it's a different story.

In the Beginning...

At first, my dad was a real success. He was fired from General Motors in Linden, New Jersey, for trying to organize a union. They said he was a wise guy, but he was just ahead of his time. Dad had a horse as big as a Clydesdale. He met with a local dairy farmer and convinced the owner to give him a home delivery route. The idea became a success as the kids told their moms to buy milk from the man with the horse and wagon. Later Dad started a used car lot in Newark, New Jersey out of an Airstream trailer. He worked that little car lot into a big car business in White Plains, New York.

It didn't take long for the new business to grow and we moved to a house in Rye, New York. The house was on almost two acres and had a small apple orchard in back. Handymen, gardeners and a live-in maid were helping Mom. We joined a country club and I had private golf lessons. Mom was driving a

Jag convertible and we were flying to Miami and taking vacations on Cape Cod and the Jersey Shore.

One day, Mom and Dad told me that the car business has been sold and we're moving to Miami. We moved with our house housekeeper, my grandmother and we took a lot of expenses with us. My parents rented a nice house in South Miami just outside of Coral Gables and I was getting ready to start high school. Mom and Dad were playing a lot of golf but Dad was not working. I thought things were going along fine. They were not.

Dad made a huge miscalculation with the finances and underestimated how much it would cost to keep up a big lifestyle. He retired too young, too early in his career, and worst of all he lost his drive and ambition. He never got back on his feet and in a few short years, the money was gone. We lost everything; Dad was mentally and physically bankrupt. I never found out why that happened.

I found myself hitchhiking to high school and cutting lawns to make lunch money. Dad cashed in his life insurance policy to finance my brother's start in college. Nothing was left to help me and we were now living one step below poor church mice. It was riches to rags, a roller coaster ride straight down. Living through the downsizing gave me motivation. I was determined not to let this happen to me when I was on my own. Nevertheless, growing up in Miami was great fun rich or poor. My attitude was positive and I had a feeling I could do well even though I was struggling in school.

I was dyslexic but had no idea. My parents did not have a clue of the problem except my grades were awful. I could only pass to the next level by taking summer classes and had to graduate high school in the summer. I enrolled in the Army as soon as I graduated but was turned down; my eyes were not adequate. I went to the University of Miami and took an aptitude test. The results came back, "You'll make a fabulous diesel mechanic, but college will be difficult if not impossible for you."

I enrolled in college night classes and felt if I could take courses I enjoyed, I could pass them. I took classes in accounting and English and even tried a drafting course. I was not sure what I wanted to do but I was sure of one thing, I did not want to be a diesel mechanic. I worked and saved for two years to get a semester paid for at the University of Tampa. It was the first time I was able to study without working full time and did well enough to earn a small scholarship, but my money ran out and I had to quit school.

Back in Miami, I found skilled Cuban refugees willing to work for small salaries to start a new life. The job market had become especially tough for the young and inexperienced. I could not find work that would pay me enough to afford a small studio apartment. It was back living with my parents. I needed to find a way to make a living and get out on my own.

My grandmother lived in Hillside, New Jersey, and offered me a room in her house. The job market had to be better in the New York area so I left Miami and started out with one hundred dollars, two pairs of jeans, a few T-shirts and a guitar. When I got to New Jersey, I didn't have a car but was able to walk to a job I found at the huge ESSO gas station in Union on Route 22 by the Garden State Parkway. I pumped gas and made change every night for weeks and weeks. Dinner was Mounds Candy Bars from the candy dispenser. I was homesick for Miami, my family, and friends. It was dark and cold in the dead of winter. I missed the sunshine. However, I was happy to have a job and be able to earn a little money. I told myself that I couldn't get much lower and it could only go up from here.

My uncle was looking out for me. He helped me get a job as a service technician at a copy machine company. It was an opportunity and I could stop pumping gas all night. I was enthusiastic and quickly worked my way up to selling copy machines and making commissions. I was good at sales and had inherited something from my dad.

By the time I was 23 I had an apartment in Montclair, a new Rocket 88 Olds convertible and enough credit to get my first American Express charge card. In those days, you really had to have good credit to get a credit card. In a few short years, I was married and able to buy and sell a house for a nice profit. We saved enough to move our family to Miami. I had gained advertising sales experience by working at Women's Wear Daily and Mademoiselle Magazine in New York.

When we got to Miami, I was able to get a start in the radio business with my advertising experience. In no time, I was earning more in radio sales in Miami than the magazine business had paid me in New York. Our expenses were low and by the time I was 28, we had two children, and a nice house. Life was good and my personal skills were making a career for me. I found myself in a new kind of management and ready to move up to bigger challenges.

I was gaining experience by doing, and learning from the street. Like most average people who achieve success, I was taking my average skills and working them overtime. Should you be smarter and more talented than average, that's a gift. However, if you *don't* master personal and communication skills, you may be throwing your gift away. Natural talents may be of little advantage without the ability to sell yourself, your ideas and the ability to influence others.

A job or working for others is what gets most people started. Some would like to skip the job part and go right on to being self-employed, own a business or even be a full time investor. However, it takes time to learn a trade or profession. It takes experience to determine *what* people want to do and importantly, what they are *capable* of doing.

Many will discover the steps to being self-employed are more difficult and demanding than a job. Owing a business more difficult yet. And Investing, while it has the halo and appeal of the Holy Grail and the most rewarding, is far and away the most difficult for the inexperienced and untrained.

Don't be so quick to hurry a process that takes time. Education, the kind you get from working with others and gaining real-life experience, is the key to long-term success.

Knowledge and experience helps you make the smart informed decisions. Working for others may be priceless education that rewards you with a paycheck as you learn.

In a society of instant gratification, jobs may seem the slow way to get wealthy and independent. But over time, jobs *you learn from* may prove to be the best opportunity and investment.

So if you don't like your job or you're just coasting along, find a better one. Don't waste your valuable time wanting to do something else. Do something else! Jobs and careers don't hold you back. It's only a *way of thinking* that stops you from moving forward.

Preface

What it Takes
to be Great

Careers are successful because of the ability to handle yourself. And others.

Being great is within reach of us all. Average intelligence and skills will do just fine. Moreover, you don't have to look like a movie star. The fact is, when you look under the covers, you see all successful people start out like everyone else. They just figure out how to become their own rainmakers. What it takes to be great is the willingness to put in the time, learn the skills and practice. Add a massive amount of persistence.

Greatness is about average people who get up the courage and energy to run at careers, advancement, putting a business together or following a dream. They *learn* how to be great after enormous effort, time and energy. Talent doesn't show up on the list as an asset until you earn it. People are not born artists, presenters, programmers, leaders, entrepreneurs or CEO's. It's what's learned after practice and drill, drill, drill like Tiger Woods pounding golf balls hours on end since he was 18 months old.

Most people simply run out of steam as the uphill climb gets steeper and the challenge gets more difficult. And that's what separates the successful from the average.

Winners get so focused on success they become blind, dense and oblivious to distractions around them and they don't know when to stop. Others are wired like a thoroughbred racehorse knowing not to quit until they cross the finish line, *ahead of everyone else.* In the meantime, the average has long since settled for getting what life dishes out and accepts fate.

What it takes to be great is almost entirely up to you and how much are you willing to push yourself. You can make yourself into whatever you want to be. How bad do you want it is the question.

Once you start to earn your stripes and prove your abilities, you have to work at becoming a brand, someone special. Your energies, skills and successes must be noticed. Like the two railroad tracks that support the great weight of trains, your success is both *what you are* and *who you are.* You need one track to support your specialized knowledge and job literacy and you need another track to carry your skills to sell yourself, your ideas and influence others.

Whether you're a salesperson, executive or entrepreneur, good communication skills are essential. Effectively dealing with people is the inside track to success so get cracking and start learning the skills to be great!

Chapter 1

How to Think-
The Successful
Leave Clues

If your mind is empty, it is always ready for anything; it is open to everything. In the beginner's mind there are many possibilities; in the expert's mind there are few.
—Shunryu Suzuki Roshi

Want to be a success? Believe in yourself and be open to change. These are the most important reasons people are successful. Does that sound easy to do? I'm sure it does because it's easy to talk about success. But creating success is not simple or easy. You'll need focus, energy, commitment, persistence and a thick skin. Your communication has to exude enthusiasm and conviction. To be a winner, you first must believe in yourself or others will not believe in you. How you think is everything.

People may have a great attitude and talk a good game, but it is only follow through that counts. Successful people work at making things happen while others talk about doing things. Leaders and experienced managers measure people by what they do, not by what they say.

My first management job was at Smith Corona Marchant in New York and I quickly got a lesson in determination. I was managing a young man and training him how to sell copy machines for our division. He did not have sales experience, but he was quick thinking and determined. Soon after he was on the job, he started showing stress. Making sales was harder then he imagined. Weeks went by and he was faced with reality, he might lose his job before he had a chance to prove himself. He was worried but continued to work with a vengeance. Every day he came in early to prepare and made more calls than everyone else, he was putting in tremendous effort.

I coached him on sales calls, "You will make sales and you're going to be a terrific salesman," I told him to keep his confidence up. "As long as you keep doing the right things and make calls on new clients, you'll be successful. It's a matter of time, just don't quit on yourself."

But more time went by and now I was getting worried. Just as I thought he might give up, he brought an order in for three copy machines. He made a big sale to an insurance company he had been working on for weeks and more orders were on the way. "Success," I thought. I'm glad he didn't give up and he finally broke the ice. I loved his determination.

Later he confided in me saying, "I was trying to look good but I couldn't. I didn't want to be a paper tiger, that's not my style. I was a nervous wreck until I made that first sale."

Once he proved to himself that he could sell, his attitude changed. He was like a golf ball bouncing in a tile bathroom.

"Now, I can feel good!" he said with enthusiasm.

Success will fix an attitude faster than anything.

To be Happy, be Productive

In the movie "Jerry Maguire," Rod has told Jerry he will keep him as his sports agent. Jerry said that's great and he was very happy. But Rod didn't think Jerry had the right attitude. Rod demanded more and more until Jerry was screaming, "Show Me the Money!" Many people are like Rod. They need to see the results or they don't believe.

Everyone has a unique viewpoint and people react to things differently. You cannot manage or help others from your own personal desires and perspective. My attitude and behavior was like a bouncing light with a lampshade on my head. But that was me, and it doesn't mean others should have my style. Over the years, I have seen sales people go from despondent to jubilant and all it took was making a sale. This taught me that while sales people were telling me they were working for the money, something else was just as important.

I noticed when sales people got commission checks, they were happy but when they got orders, they were elated. It's the chicken or the egg theory. You can argue the merits but what comes first has little relevance. The common denominator for a good attitude is a sense of well-being and the feeling of accomplishment. Nothing can replace that. People are at their best when they are productive and in a good environment.

In 1981, I was managing KPOI FM radio, 98Rock in Honolulu. I had just changed the station to a new format when I hired Lee "Baby" Sims to do an on air show. It was sheer dumb luck on my part. Lee was living in Honolulu and coasting along. He was a great radio talent and taking some time off to live in paradise. However, I think he was bored with the good weather and wanted to be on the radio to keep busy. He came to the station to see if we needed any help. As our station was just getting under way, we didn't have the money to pay him what he was worth.

But lucky for us, Lee didn't have many options. Even with his talent and experience, if he wanted to do a rock 'n' roll radio show in Hawaii, we were his best option. So, we agreed to agree. Lee would do morning drive and I told him he could do the show his way as long as he didn't put the radio station license in jeopardy. I figured it would have been impossible to manage him anyway so we made it easy for Lee to work at the station.

Lee went on the air. It took only a couple of hours before the other DJ's realized Lee had a lot to teach them. Many DJ's got in the radio business learning to read the "liner cards." But without training and coaching, it's hard to develop good communication skills.

Don't be Afraid to Innovate

One morning, I'm in the office early. I have the radio on in the background and I hear a new voice on the air I don't recognize. Lee had a guest in the studio and they are giggling and laughing in between the music. It sounded like a couple of middle age guys on a hard rock radio station giving away bags of cookies. I said to my self, "This is bizarre."

I bolted out of my chair, ran down to the studios and looked in the glass windows. There was this tall distinguished looking black guy standing next to Lee. He was wearing a huge Panama hat and had on a bright Hawaiian shirt. They were on the air talking to listeners and giving away little bags of Famous Amos cookies. I realized that *was* Famous Amos. The cookie man was giving away his cookies.

I walked in the studio and introduced myself. I asked Lee to step outside the studio for a second between songs.

"Lee," I said, "are you nuts? This is hard rock radio; we're playing melt down music for young men. Are you telling me our listeners are chocolate chip cookies fans? You must be kidding me!"

"No," said Lee. And walked back in the studio.

Lee wasn't kidding. It wasn't the cookies; it was what they were doing and what they weren't supposed to be doing on the radio. I thought this is either going to work because it's so bizarre it's brilliant, or we were about to blow up our morning show and all our marketing efforts.

Our ratings were low enough at that point we didn't have a lot of risk so I thought, let's see where this goes. In time, we will find what works and what does not; the report card was all in the ratings. The morning show got more bizarre and the stunts were off the wall. I kept my distance as best I could but I did a lot of praying and hand wringing. Our listeners would tell us if they liked what we were doing. And apparently, they did like Lee. The morning show rocked to a 15.7 share of men, the highest FM morning ratings ever reported in the Honolulu market.

Lee's unique way of thinking made his show a success. The others on the staff were focused on the music. Lee was only *playing* the music and called the songs nails in a board. "I just drive them in," Lee said.

His secret was to tell stories on the air and hold everyone's attention. Listeners were forced to stay on the station to hear him finish his stories, the music was an afterthought. I began to wonder if we should have any music at all, Lee was far more entertaining. He was a natural talent.

Some rules for morning shows are no indication of what would or would not work. Success is more about individuals and personalities. My thinking and inexperience was the problem. I was determined to learn more. Creativity and innovation is not in hardbound books, I was guilty of jumping to conclusions.

Think Slow in a Hurry

People can think too fast and come to conclusions without really thinking. Those that value cleverness over smart thinking or wisdom are not as intelligent as they appear. Slow minds do not mean poor thinking; actually, it's the opposite. We are taught in school to finish timed tests and are graded on how quickly we can recall information. But that has little to do with how you think.

"Act quickly, think slowly," says an old Greek proverb. It takes time to digest information and develop clear thinking.

If your career depends on your thinking, don't be in a hurry to think your way through problems. A sense of urgency is important to get things accomplished. That is different from a commitment to a quick fix for a problem. That old turtle keeps winning races. The rabbit is too quick for his own good.

> Fast is fine, but accuracy is everything.
> **—Wyatt Earp**
> Gunfighter and frontier marshal

I got to know Famous Amos. He was a regular guest on the 98Rock morning show. We called him Fame and he brought huge bags of cookies for everyone at the station. He loved the islands and lived in Lanaki on the Windward side of Oahu. The Famous Amos cookie empire was being built across the country and Hawaii was home base.

"Where did you learn about marketing and promotion for your cookie business?" I asked.

"I worked for the William Morris Agency in Los Angeles for 7 years during the 1960s. We worked with rock 'n' roll bands and music talent across the country and I was able to learn about marketing and promotions. When I got in the cookie business, I was able to use a lot of the ideas from first hand experience. I give cookies a personality and created a brand," Fame told me.

Several years later, I left the islands. I took an opportunity to work with Viacom and moved to Washington, DC as manager of WMZQ FM country radio. I later moved to New York to become President of the Viacom Radio Group.

When I met with Fame again he told me a story. It was about his cookie business and what happened since I left Hawaii. Fame told me he got to his goal of a $10,000,000 company. But the fame and celebrity went to his head.

"I wasn't listening to people in my company. I was Famous Amos and I became this character. I didn't pay attention to the business and I lost control. I lost my investors. I lost the company and even lost my name, 'Famous Amos,' in a lawsuit."

It was hard to believe what I was hearing. Outsiders had gotten control of his company. Fame was not paying attention to the business. He had trusted others to run the company for him and it proved to be a hard lesson to learn, "Trust everyone, but brand your cattle."

Believe In Yourself

In spite of his problems, Fame told me he wrote a book, *Man with No Name: Turn Lemons into Lemonade,* started a muffin company "The Uncle *Noname* Cookie Company," and was giving speeches on adversity and attitude.

His latest business, "Chip & Cookie," is a retail cookie and a bookstore business for kids. The lesson from Fame is one we don't need to experience to understand. None of us needs a catastrophic failure to test our mantle. What makes this story important is self-confidence. Fame believed in himself. Most people would have been defeated and mentally bankrupt for life after that tragic misstep. But Fame took it in stride and said, "Next!"

Where is Your Thinking?

Success is a way of thinking and most people are in one of three places: The unsuccessful are thinking survival, the average person is thinking how to maintain the status quo and the leaders and winners are thinking about moving forward and creating success. But for every ten people you meet only *one* will become truly successful.

Those who do not believe in themselves will hesitate to take risks. Without risks, success will be limited. People should trust their instincts more; it could be the best thinking they are ever going to get. In school, we are taught to be good and do as we're told. This is not a recipe for innovation and creativity. Successful people and entrepreneurs are out on a limb thinking opportunity, not clinging to the tree and being conservative. Winners and successful people make the hard decisions once they have the information while most people stay on the safer path. The greater logic and most people say be careful but the smart thinking of the successful says, *take the calculated risks.*

If you look for support from others because you don't trust your instincts, be aware *consensus thinking leans towards safety*. Group thinking may distract you from taking calculated risks; a consensus might not make good leadership or entrepreneurial calls.

Use Both Sides

Right-brain thinking opens the door to the creative and innovative process. This side of your thinking is also drive, passion, persistence and emotion. And it is this side of your brain that helps your think past normal and average.

The left-brain is the logic side of your thinking. The analytical side interprets data and information you need while keeping you from being a bag of scrambled emotions. The left-brain gives you the good grades in school; it is the same kind of thinking accountants need to do their jobs.

You need both sides of your thinking to maximize potential. Those that did well in school will not necessary do well in the competitive business world.

In school, we are taught to have answers. But in real life and business, we have multiple-choice questions and our problems have multiple answers.

Clear thinking needs to be devoid of emotions. If you are tied to your emotional side, you may never rid yourself of old thinking. You will be too attached to see new opportunities. And if you only focused on your logic side, you might overanalyze things and mentally paralyze yourself from taking action. You need passion for drive and motivation as that is what gets you moving. Emotions and logic go hand in hand; one should not overbalance the other. Use both left and right brain thinking, one side helps you make decisions and the other side helps you take action.

Bee Thinking Precession

Think one thing and something else comes of it. And sometimes it is something unexpected. R. Buckminster Fuller called it precession and it affects bodies in motion on *other* bodies in motion. The principle repeats itself over and over in nature, science, and business. Its doing things and thinking one way that leads you to another.

Bees and flowers are a metaphor to show how this works. The honeybee finds flowers and crawls inside. The bee is after the nectar to make honey. But in the process, the bee is accidentally dusted with pollen. He goes to the next flower for more nectar but he is actually cross-pollinating another flower. The bee thinks his job is to gather honey. However, his *purpose* is to pollinate flowers.

Apple computer had been in the computer and software business since the 1970s before it created the iPod music player and iTunes software. Someone was awake and thinking out of the box when they saw an opportunity to get in the music industry. Apple developed the new hardware and software to both play music and get music royalties from downloading songs. Just because Apple was in the computer and software business, it did not stop them from thinking and doing something new. The iPod was a precessional effect; the thinking came from something Apple was already doing. It just took them in a different direction and Apple, again, reinvented itself.

David Saperstein was General Manager of a car dealership in Baltimore, Maryland when we first met and started doing business. I traded lease cars with David for radio station advertising and it was a win/win proposition. But he saw a new way to trade with radio stations. Rush hour was awful; people tied up in traffic jams and had no way of knowing how to avoid the problem. It would be a major benefit to radio stations if listeners could hear live traffic reports. So David founded Metro Traffic, a news and information company that supplied live traffic reports to radio stations without the sky-high costs of maintaining helicopters and airplanes. Metro Traffic was trading live information for radio station advertising. The new and unique concept grew Metro Traffic into a phenomenal nationwide success with precessional thinking.

Fame was in the talent and promotion agency business working with rock 'n' roll music, bands and talent, and a long way from the chocolate chip cookies business. However, he saw his promotional and marketing experience could also sell cookies and the gourmet cookie industry was born. It took a good recipe for cookies but the marketing and branding of "Famous Amos" was the new thinking and key to success.

Keep Things Simple

No law prevents you from thinking new and unique ideas. It's only you who can stop yourself from different thinking. The best ideas may be right in front of you and can come from your own experience. Do not be afraid to innovate. Be different. If you follow the path everyone else is on, it is probably a path to mediocrity.

It takes smart thinking to make things less confusing and manageable. People tend to get caught up in the minutia of their ideas and often miss the boat and the big picture. Over thinking may complicate and cloud real issues and get you off track. Keep focused on the goal and do not mistake movement for achievement. Making distinctions of what to focus on is critical to how you think. When things are simple, it is easier to decide what direction to go.

> A perfection of means, and confusion of aims, seems to be our main problem. Any intelligent fool can make things bigger and more complex... It takes a touch of genius - and a lot of courage to move in the opposite direction. Everything should be as simple as it is, but not simpler.
> **—Albert Einstein**

Secrets to Successful Thinking:
- **Be receptive to change, things will happen**
- **Don't be afraid to innovate or be different, your ideas may be far better than others**
- **Believe in yourself, trust your instincts**
- **Paradigms may hold you back, be sure you are looking ahead**
- **Precession may lead you to new ideas and opportunities you never dreamed of**
- **Beware of negative people and environments**
- **Develop self-confidence and reinforce it with positive thinking**
- **Act on visions and thoughts, you can always ask for forgiveness later if your wrong**
- **Think slowly and collect your thoughts, fast is for racecars**

- **Keep emotions out of your rational thinking and use logic**
- **Use emotions to drive ambitions and take the calculated risks**
- **Keep It Simple! Don't complicate thinking**

In school, they teach you critical thinking and how to find correct answers but in life and business, you need creative thinking as you are looking for opportunities:

> Never let schooling interfere with education.
> **—Mark Twain**

Looking Ahead

Companies will not have a safe easy road to follow and this affects everyone. Being cheaper or more productive by itself is not a guarantee it will beat fast track global competition. Ramping up profits and bottom lines through productivity and downsizing moves in cycles. The future of global competition however, is about creative and innovating thinking. Innovation trumps efficiency.

In a speech to the Harvard Business School Class of 2005, the CEO of GE gave advice for the future to the graduating students:

> The crisis in corporate America today is a little bit about governance and a lot about a rampant lack of innovation. Take personal risks rather than blindly follow the road most popular at the moment. You have to find your own path.
> **—Jeff Immelt**
> CEO and Chairman of General Electric

As we move forward, we need to create better environments for workers and management to focus on innovation and creativity. Companies that share wealth with workers create better opportunities for themselves. And companies with less emphasis on hierarchy and political order will do better in the competitive global marketplace.

Forget Playing it Safe, Go For It

Global competition is not about safety; it is about winning new markets and customers and thinking differently. A company not focused on improving itself will have learning experiences in its future. And people in careers do not need me to tell them "job safety" is an oxymoron as global competition churns jobs and the economy.

We have less safety in faster moving times but we also have new opportunities. Companies will have little choice but to move faster than ever before and think more like entrepreneurs. Focus your thinking on new opportunities as the world changes.

> Opportunity brings risk. Take control or you may become unable to manage or lead effectively.

Companies with the best relationships with their employees will meet the challenge of competition and be stronger to defend their position. Innovation will be the best offense and defense a company can have.

How you think gives you confidence to take action. However, it is also how you think that holds you back and robs you of success. Anytime you take a step forward, you are taking a risk. You must trust your ideas, believe in yourself, and be open to change.

I rate enthusiasm and a positive attitude above professional skills. What good is brilliant thinking if you don't do anything with it? Times ahead are exciting in a new world of competition. Workers and companies need to focus on creativity, ingenuity and innovation as we head into an economy of imagination. A new style of management will lead an enlightened work force. People with vision and good personal skills will rise to the top and become our new leaders.

Steps to Success

- **Keep Things Simple**
- **How You Think Is Everything, Use Both Sides Of Your Brain**
- **Creativity Is Not In The Rule Book**
- **Confidence Is Essential, Trust Your Instincts**
- **Don't Rush To Judgment, Keep An Open Mind**
- **You Must Take Calculated Risks To Create Success**

Chapter 2

Communication- Getting Points Across

Developing excellent communication skills is absolutely essential to effective leadership. The leader must be able to share knowledge and ideas to transmit a sense of urgency and enthusiasm to others. If a leader can't get a message across clearly and motivate others to act on it, then having a message doesn't even matter.

—Gilbert Amelio
CEO National Semiconductor

The brightest or most capable do not always end up in the corner office. It is people with communication skills that go to the head of the class. They are most admired, make more money, and attract the opportunities. The higher you go in a company, the more critical communication skills become. Effective speaking in business is no longer a plus. It's expected. Selling ideas and influencing others is essential in today's competitive world

Communicating is a learned skill, not born talent. Your learn how to communicate from your environment. The workplace, friends, school, parents, and media influence your style. However, like professional athletes, successful people in business work to improve their natural skills.

Words Are Power

The spoken word is more powerful than the written word; it is an intellectual and behavioral process. We speak with the ability to evoke emotions of enthusiasm, sadness, anger, and excitement. And if we do not communicate effectively, we can put people to sleep. When you hear the spoken voice and see power and emotion in people, you get real communication.

Luckily, you do not need a professional radio or TV announcer's voice. You don't need a good physical appearance to communicate and speak well. However, you do need to use clear thoughts and well-formed sentences. Communicating is not about slickness, it is about how clearly you can express ideas and thoughts. You need to be real and project passion about your ideas. Simple and clear is what makes great speakers and good communicators.

Less Is More

The quality of information we communicate is how people judge us, not the quantity. It is clarity we need but we get a lot of the opposite. People may be artful and deceitful at making simple things difficult to understand. Those who are able to *explain concepts in simple terms are the gifted communicators.* You must be able to explain your visions clearly.

I once worked for a manager who had the notion that effective communication was speaking more than the other person did. He thought good speech was the ability to say more and wear the other person out. If he disagreed with you, he would just keep talking as he felt he had the power of persuasion in his speaking. Luckily, he had a great bubbly personality so it was hard to disagree with him but the point of speaking more and saying less was apparent. When he stopped talking, you wondered what was said or if it even mattered. It is what you say and how you say it, not how much you say.

The Gettysburg address was only 286 words. Winston Churchill's "blood, sweat, and tears" speech to the British Parliament was 627 words and lasted only 6 minutes. You do not want people to think, "Why doesn't he just tell us what matters and get it over with?" Choose your words carefully, edit your thoughts and say what needs to be said.

Whether you sell advertising, consult a business, or teach students, speaking is more powerful and effective when it is focused and concise. John F. Kennedy's, "My fellow Americans, ask not what your country can do for you; ask what you can do for your country," or Ronald Reagan telling Gorbachev to, "Tear down this wall," were brilliant focused thoughts that had a point with very few words.

Hearing Is Not Listening

Ever notice that people have an answer to your thoughts before you finish a sentence? That is because people talk at 150 to 180 words a minute yet hear and understand words spoken many times faster. People easily race ahead of thoughts in conversation and many are only listening to reply, not to understand. People listen passively out of habit and are only interested in what *they* have to say. Passive listeners rarely acknowledge what others have said.

I would hear the same comments over and over, "Considering we're in the communication business, we sure are lousy communicators!" The broadcasting business even though it is an industry of communicators has the same problems as other industries. Few work hard at becoming active listeners.

When people talk, listen completely. Most people never listen.

—Ernest Hemingway

The successful make a major distinction between hearing and listening: much of our success comes from knowledge and information we get from others. Winners do not want to miss important communications and have learned how to be active listeners. Active listening requires concentration and focus and that is what enables you to comprehend more than spoken words.

What Is Active Listening?

Experts claim only 7% of communication is verbal, 35% is tone and emotion. The rest is body language. *The majority of communication is not spoken.* When someone is speaking with folded arms, laughing, grinning, starting to pace around, winking, growling or raising their eyebrows, they are telling you more than they are saying. It's up to you to listen. Active listening is both listening to what is said but watching and hearing emotions. Many subtleties are not the spoken word *but are said in communication.*

> The most important thing in communications is hearing what isn't said.
> —**Peter Drucker**

It's Never the Story, It's Always the Emotion

Communication may be more than the spoken word. Listen to what people *say* but look for the communication of how people *feel.* The intensity of emotions will tell you what people are really saying. A hypochondriac had his tombstone in Key West, Florida read:

> I told you I was sick.
> —**B. Pearl Roberts**

Listening actively enables a better environment for others to communicate with you. The more attention you give, the more others will give you in return. People enjoy speaking to others that are interested in what they are saying. An active listener spends more time listening than talking.

Communication skills are a tool. It is how you sell ideas and influence people. Leaders focus on improving their communication ability. Some attend special classes while others may have private coaches. You cannot lead if you cannot influence others. Generating enthusiasm and a sense of urgency is critical.

Sell Your Image, Sell Your Ideas

A strong self-image is vital, the data and information you possess will not guarantee your success. It is your ability to *sell your ideas* that matters. Most people hate to think of themselves as salesmen, but love to think of themselves as communicators. However, the secret is it takes *salesmanship* to be successful. Even your dentist is figuring out ways to sell you more services and products from whiter teeth to better breath.

People Hate Salesmen Almost as Much as Lawyers

Selling has a perception problem. Over the years, Hollywood and the media have painted sales people with negative images. Rarely do we see positive images of sales professionals. We have been programmed to think of the profession filled with inept unscrupulous people. While this makes for good entertainment, it does not reflect reality.

Just Learn the Skills

You do not have to choose a sales career and you do not have to be a salesman. However, if you hold a negative image of selling it may influence your subconscious mind and your best efforts may be held back. Successful people sell ideas, concepts and motivation to others; it's an important and integral part of communicating. If your concept of selling is non-stop blabbermouth talking, that is not selling and will only risk relationships and annoy others.

A Quick Sales Meeting for Non-Sales People

Three elements critical to professional sales:
- Be a good listener, it is more important than talking.
- Show interest in helping others.
- Think positively and be passionate about your ideas.

These sales skills are also the traits of the most respected and powerful people. Presidents, CEO's and leaders live by these key rules.

Selling is showing passion and enthusiasm for your ideas. When energy and enthusiasm levels are low, you cannot project excitement and a sense of urgency. To project your ideas, you will need enough natural emotion and conviction that others may see. A PMA, "Positive Mental Attitude" is critical.

> You can have brilliant ideas, but if you can't get them across, your ideas won't get you anywhere.
>
> **—Lee Iacocca**

Are You Cool? That's Not Always a Hot Idea

If you think "being cool" is not showing emotions and enthusiasm, you are likely to be the loser. People that would rather be cool than make a sale or improve a career are the good-looking suits going nowhere. If you want your career in high gear, you need to sell yourself, your ideas, and concepts.

Thinking bold is not speaking loudly or unprofessionally; *it's all about style*. Good ideas combined with energy and emotions are what it takes to convince others to your way of thinking. Selling is more common sense and natural communication than many realize. Learn how to sell yourself with honesty and integrity and show excitement, energy and enthusiasm. The concept of selling is misunderstood and unfortunately for many, it is exactly the skill needed to develop a career.

> Before you can inspire with emotion, you must be swamped with it yourself. Before you can move their tears, your own must flow. To convince them, you must yourself believe.
>
> **—Winston Churchill**

Communicating with People Effectively

Ideas and concepts sharpen communication; little things can have impact. Communication is active listening and getting ideas across to others, but it is a two way street. It's not only what you say and communicate; it's how *others* perceive you. Be sensitive to what motivates people and you will be able to lead and influence more effectively. The following ideas can help you position your thoughts and actions:

Use Your Body

Eye contact, facial expressions, body and posture are all part of communication. Speak with clarity and try to say more with fewer words. Take a breath, use pauses for emphasis. Give people a chance to respond to what you say and do not babble on and overrun your good ideas and thoughts. You should never use a continuous monotone voice; vary your loudness, pitch and tone. Exude energy, enthusiasm and confidence when appropriate. Your body dominates you; it is your overwhelming feature. Use all your personal impact to get your ideas and points across.

Find Common Ground

Active listeners plan a response *after* others finish
speaking. Avoid the trap of interrupting, be sure what
others have said. Listen and understand people so you can
position the conversation to a middle or common ground.
This common ground enables you to talk from the same
viewpoint or perspective of others. It shows you understand
what is being said and it makes communication easier to
continue from both sides. Pace the speaking tone to be
compatible with others or they may tune you out.

Acknowledge What Others Say

When you acknowledge others, *you are enhancing your
own position.* Nothing is more important to others than
hearing their own names and being understood. When
people speak, *acknowledge what they are saying, show
interest and respond.* This is much more powerful than
people realize. Being receptive to other points of view is
paramount. Ask questions, stay alert and suspend
judgment. Do not jump to conclusions before you are sure
you understand what others are saying.

Respect Different Viewpoints

Do not listen just to get information to support your ideas
or points of view. It shows disrespect, and stops you from
seeing things from a different perspective. Everyone is
entitled to his or her point of view, right or wrong.
Listening actively only means you are trying to understand.
Paying attention demonstrates you are respectful enough to
hear others' ideas and opinions but it does not mean you
have to agree with them. Business relationships are built on
common ground *and* diversity. Different ideas and opinions
create synergy, the foundation of all business. Don't try to

make others conform to all of your ideas and you will earn new friends and respect.

Stay on Topic

Good communicators do not change the subject of conversation in mid-stream; they wait for the other person to complete the thought or idea. If you change the subject before others are finished, you are saying, "I don't care what you just said" or "I have something more important to say than you do." Change the subject before its time and you will likely lose the rest of the conversation or communication.

Don't Trump Others

"I can top that" puts you in a poor position. When someone tells you they just got back from London, you can say, "Where did you stay, what did you do?" Or you can say, "We went from London to Santorini in the Greek Islands," to top what was just said. Do not try and top the conversation or people will be wishing they were anywhere other than talking to you. To be interesting, be interested and add to the conversation. Acknowledge what is said.

Raise the Gradient Slowly

Remember the story of the frog and the boiling water. If you put a frog in a pot of hot boiling water, it will jump out. But if you put a frog in a pot of cool water and slowly turn up the heat, the frog will slowly get accustomed to the temperature rising. The frog never feels the heat rising. That heat rising is the *gradient.* Slowly raise intensity and ideas when you meet people, *or they will jump out of the pot.* Until you understand where others are coming from, raise the gradient slowly or you can wind up shooting yourself in the foot and scaring people away.

Never Talk in Absolutes

Talking in absolutes is a subtle turn off and you can easily avoid this mistake. However, many are oblivious they are even doing it. When you speak, use open terms. Let others have their own opinion and thoughts. Speaking in absolute terms ends the communication as you have spoken for others. You never *know* what others are thinking; you can only *assume* what they are thinking. Speak in terms of, "I have an idea, let's...." or "We should look at this problem and see if we can..." Do not start thoughts with definitive answers, "I know we all feel this way." That is not a good opener for conversation and shows you are insensitive to others. It's easy to change the tone and positioning. "Some of us feel this way," works every time and makes your point.

Look to Resolve Differences

Be conscious of compromising people when you speak, it creates a win-lose situation. Make it a habit to create alternatives or new viewpoints when you have disagreements. Belligerence is a bad tactic to resolve things. If you win a point or discussion, leave something on the table so you can build relationships. When you compromise people, especially in front of others, you may win the battle, but you will lose the war. Find points you can mutually agree on.

Watch Your Temper

With a bad temper, people under you will be afraid of you. Superiors will be nervous to have you in a position of authority. Bad tempers are not good for business and a quick tongue and temper can be the "Kiss of Death" for a career. Your good qualities are immediately preempted when tempers are hot as you are communicating to everyone, "I'm out of control," and "You can't trust me."

Keep Your Ego in Check

Everyone needs a strong ego; it is the critical edge for speakers and communicators. You cannot think of yourself as insignificant if you want to become a mountain of strength. However, if this great strength is overused, it can become an Achilles heel. When egos are out of control, it is difficult to get honest communication as you have put others on defense. Show humility, affinity and compassion. The more authority you have, the more careful you have to watch your speech and behavior. Big egos out of control are shown the door as soon as others can open it.

Electronic and Digital Communication

With new technologies, many use blogging, text messaging, pagers and email. The computer keyboard is an important way to say things and communicate. More and more people are doing "stuff" not face to face. Many successful people use the computer as a medium but they have already mastered the skills of verbal communication.

But others with less experience may not have the communication skills and body language important for good speaking. The electronic media has made it easy to let personal skills lapse or not be developed. People say things behind a keyboard they will never say in person. The point is we do not *speak* electronically. "LOL" (laugh out loud) or "YMMV" (your mileage may vary) is not real life language.

Electronic shortcuts will short-circuit your career if you let electronic skills replace your communication ability. Talent will not mean a lot if you cannot hold a good conversation. Be sure you do not replace electronic communication for real world speaking. Learn to do both well.

Build a Strong Foundation

Technical job competence is not the big roadblock in a career. For most people, it is being a good communicator. You do not have to be a professional presenter however; you *must* learn to be an effective speaker. In today's competitive world, being a good communicator is a must-have skill.

Big company or small, the ability to communicate well is the ability to talk to customers and work with clients. Selling your ideas and yourself is what creates success. The higher you go in your career, the more important these skills become.

Leaders and successful people build their careers with strong communication skills and you can do the same. It just takes practice, effort and an awareness of how important it is to be a good communicator. Sell your ideas with optimism and enthusiasm and you are on your way to success.

How do I put my communication skills to work? Read ahead how blind men try to understand elephants and a frisky frog teaches negotiating principles in poetry.

Steps to Success

- **The Secret To Communication: Listening**
- **Pay Attention To Everything When People Speak, Important Details Are Often Spoken In Emotions**
- **Clarity Is Power: Speak Less - Say More**
- **Good Communicators Move Up The Ladder Fast**
- **Brilliant Ideas Go Nowhere If You Can't Get Them Across**

Chapter 3

Negotiating-
Rules of the Game

The one sure way to conciliate a tiger is to allow oneself to
be devoured.

—**Konrad Adenauer** (1876-1967)

John Godfrey Saxe, 1816-1887, made a famous Chinese
parable into a poem. The story from the Han Dynasty 202 BC:

The Blind Men and the Elephant

A long time ago in India, six blind men lived in a village.
One day, the blind men heard an elephant had wandered into
town. These blind men had no idea what an elephant was, so
they decided to go for a visit. Even though they couldn't see
the elephant, they would be able to feel it and discover what it
was.

The first blind man felt the tail and said, "I found a rope!"

The second said, "It's a tree!" as he touched the elephant's knee.

"It's a big fan!" said the third blind man as he touched one of the elephant's ears.

The fourth man found a squirming trunk and said, "It must be a snake!"

The fifth touched the sharp tusk and said, "It's very much like a spear!"

And the sixth blind man said, "No, no, you're all wrong, it must be a wall!" as he ran his hands over the elephant's body.

The men continued to argue over what the elephant was. A wise man walking by overheard the discussion.

"What is the matter?" the wise man asked.

"We all see the elephant differently, and we can't agree on what it is," the blind men replied.

The wise man thought about the problem and said, "As each of you has touched a different part of the elephant, each of you has a different understanding of what it is. You're all right, and you're all wrong. The elephant is larger and more complex than any one of you realize."

What You See Depends

Each of us creates our own versions of reality. We see things through our paradigms and filters of experience and interests. We are blind to the totality of what we deal with. We often make conclusions from images that are subjective at best. It's human nature to make judgments, even on partial information.

Negotiating is like the blind men understanding the elephant. Everyone negotiates but few gain enough insight to understand all of it. For most people, negotiating is difficult. It's like speaking in public; the thought of it turns stomachs and creates anxiety. Asking for a raise or negotiating money is at the top of the discomfort zone. Some won't negotiate for fear of being labeled aggressive or pushy. Others fear confronting authority or upsetting the status quo.

Many fears associated with negotiating are from old paradigms. As companies move away from a hierarchical management style, they will adjust to a new workforce and competitive environment. The manager's job will be less about authority. Boundaries between managers and workers will blur, more responsibilities will be in the hands of workers.

Companies Want More and So Do Workers

Companies are asking workers for more productivity but they will be hoping for more innovation and creativity as well. Workers in turn will have new opportunities. As jobs and boundaries change, people need to become better negotiators to gain benefits for their efforts. Those who create more value can expect more in return. But don't think companies will roll out the red carpet for your achievements. You'll have to negotiate your way to success.

Standing up for yourself will not make enemies or bad impressions. Likewise, it will not reflect badly on you. To the contrary, it shows self-worth and a positive attitude. If you get labeled as weak or a pushover, you'll have a tough time overcoming that image.

Negotiating is Not Litigating

Litigating is a formal legal process. It deals with lawsuits, claims, and arguments that usually end with a winner and a loser.

Negotiating is a process to create co-operation and agreement. It takes many forms. We use negotiations to set schedules and priorities, create contracts, settle differences, establish prices, set standards, buy things and sell things. Anything can be negotiated.

In successful negotiations, everyone wins something but no one has victory over the other. The goal is to manage conflict, hostilities and disagreements. Successful negotiations create a better environment to get along with bosses, people at work, friends and family.

No one is born with negotiating skills but with practice and experience, you can greatly improve them. Negotiating impacts every aspect of your life, it's how you express your desires, wants and needs. If you don't negotiate, your silence can mean you've negotiated your rights and opinions away. Silence is a negotiating tactic. By not voicing your thoughts or position, it will imply approval or agreement. When you are silent, be sure that is what you mean.

Business is Not Fair or Democratic

People rely on negotiating skills to influence others, recruit people, and make business deals work. With experience almost everyone comes to the same conclusion, *"You get what you negotiate, not what you deserve."* Business is not fair or democratic; it's an endless opportunity that you work at.

People in executive positions or high levels of management negotiate day in and day out on countless issues. They also use the skills for personal advancement, recognition, and pay issues. They see negotiation as a *"must have"* skill for their careers. Yet many in key positions are oblivious to the fact that others do not use negotiation to their advantage. So, they  are often surprised and blindsided when good people quit without expressing they have problems or issues. Right or wrong, many executives assume if workers have something important to discuss, it will be aired. Busy executives don't look to find new problems and if things are not brought up, everything is assumed to be working well. Never assume others know your concerns or issues. Speak up.

When you skillfully negotiate, it's perceived as strength and a talent. Managers and leaders negotiate for themselves every day and most will understand when others do the same. The way to get respect from leaders is through your efforts and behavior. Even if issues you negotiate don't work out your way, you're better off trying than being silent. In almost every case, if you don't win your point, you win respect if you negotiate properly. Squeaky wheels get the grease, not quiet ones that appear to be running smoothly.

The Sign on the Wall

I was working in Hawaii and needed an attorney to help me with copyrights and contract agreements. I asked some business friends for recommendations and Stuart's name came up. I called him and he said, "My office is just up the street from you so come on over." I met him in his office and saw four-foot high stacks of legal files on the floor. The file cabinets were filled and overflowing. The office had the feel of an old worn shoe. I figured I was in good hands; it looked like he had plenty of clients. He said, "Sit, let's talk."

As we worked together, he was organized and thorough. Detailed questions led to more questions. Everything connected with my concerns was a question. We spent the afternoon together until he finally knew as much about my issues as I did. All the time we talked, he was taking notes and writing on his legal pads.

His desk was facing out from a wall and I was sitting across from him. When he moved his chair, I noticed a small sign on the wall.

"Tell me about that sign," I asked.

He said that most people don't prepare as much as they should. And that's exactly why we will. The sign is a constant reminder for me:

The Will to Win is to Prepare

The odds of winning are in proportion to the effort you are willing to put in. Stuart told me he was preparing mentally and physically for the Ironman Triathlon World Championships on the Island of Hawaii. He told me it would take over 20 weeks of intense preparation to even be able to finish the race. I thought about that and realized the sign had real meaning for his work, and his life.

When I left Stuart's office, I knew he was a good find for me. The knowledge and information we covered was important but not being prepared would have made the information useless. Negotiating is not like poker where bluffing is a skill. In negotiations, you have to know your stuff and prepare yourself.

You also consider alternatives in case things don't go your way. You run scenarios of win, lose or draw. Preparation will not guarantee success but it sure beats any alternatives. Stuart helped me learn a valuable lesson and from that point on, any meetings or issues that I had to deal with, I would do my homework. Being prepared gives you confidence and somehow it seems the harder you work, the luckier you get.

Interviewing is a Form of Negotiating

Interviews are negotiations. I have interviewed people for all types of jobs and made many interview presentations. I discovered an important secret. People wing negotiations and interviews all the time. Many do not prepare beyond a clean shirt and an attitude. Make this secret your opportunity.

Many people behind the desk have little time to polish interview skills and often are not as prepared as you assume they would be. The rule is, **never assume anything**. When you interview you can expect a list of questions. But after that, you may get a lot of winging. How the interview goes is more up to you than you realize, expect more from yourself than the people interviewing you.

Put yourself in the position of the person you're meeting, what would you be asking? What would be the important issues? List questions you think *the interviewer is concerned about* as well as what you need to discover. Bring a brief or folder to hold your written questions and pull it out during the interview. It shows you've prepared yourself, not that you have a poor memory.

When you are prepared, you are ready to fill the void or vacuum of the interviewer who may not be prepared.

Most people doing the interviewing are happy to have a live wire thinking and asking questions. The critical point to interviewing and negotiating:

> **Who Is Best Prepared and**
> **Asks the Most Relevant Questions**
> **Will Likely Control the Meeting!**

The interview is learning about the job. The least important is your needs. No one cares about what you want, don't take it personally. People care about what they need and *that is what you pay attention to.*

You will not get a job because you need one but you will have many job offers if you can help others. If you win the job and the offer is not good, go back to the discussion table and sell your skills and assets again. Don't give in to the first offer if you're not comfortable with the agreement. It might be a test to see how strong your resolve is.

You Never Know

When you interview, think of every opportunity as having huge potential and being a fabulous job. You never know when a new Microsoft will be in the making and you're sitting in front of the next Bill Gates. Always run 110% and prepare the best you can. Go to the Internet and Google or Yahoo the company. Learn about the industry, find trade journals to read and call friends to see if they know anyone working in the company.

When you are prepared, you are probably stronger and better off than you realize. This is especially true when you're compared to others who have not prepared. Remember the story of the grizzly bear in the woods. You don't have to outrun the bear. You just have to outrun the other people.

A Tale of Two Frogs

Negotiating is not a list or series of steps you can follow; you need to set up a platform you can work from. One frog shows us an important negotiating strategy:

Two frogs fell into a deep cream bowl,
One was an optimistic soul,
But the other took a gloomy view,
We shall drown he cried, without more adieu!

So with a last despairing cry,
He flung up his legs and said "goodbye"

Said the frog with a merry grin,
I can't get out, but I won't give in,
I'll just swim around till my strength is spent,
Then I will die the more content.

Bravely he swam till it did seem,
His struggling began to churn the cream,
On top of the butter at last he stepped,
And out of the bowl at last he leapt.

What of the moral? 'Tis easily found,
If you can't get out... keep swimming around!

Negotiating is art, not science. Emotions and egos are a perfect setup for spontaneously unpredictable things to happen. *Be prepared to be surprised.* You are looking to get yourself into the best position to win or take a pass.

Setting Up Your Platform

Make your platform of ideas and positions support what you want to accomplish. More often than not, the winner will be the one with the best skills, not the best position. Negotiating "Rules of the game" are non-existent; they are made up as you go along. Your priorities must be set so you can concentrate and follow the "game." Do not get lost in what was "supposed" to be.

Think of a negotiation as a game of football. You see the goal line but you're going to have a hard time trying to make a beeline for it. It might take yard after yard of grinding effort to make progress or it can happen on one big play. Success may well depend on how prepared you are and how you think on your feet.

A classic position of negotiators is to have an attitude, it's "only a game." A game has less importance than real life since you can stop playing any time and walk away. It can be intimidating to face an attitude like this, but don't let it make you defensive; it's a ploy. People are only at the negotiating table because they think they have something to gain or win. Arrogance and aggressive behavior in negotiations is a weak position and good negotiators will see right through it. Hot air does not solve problems. Don't be too powerful for your own good and never underestimate your opposition.

Think Like Colombo but Don't Dress Like Him

Colombo from the TV series won cases. He appeared to be a scatter-brained, frumpy, cigar smoking, disheveled hayseed. But his appearance was deceiving and hid a brilliant cat-and-mouse player. The other side underestimated his prowess and abilities as he went after details and mechanics of the mind. He never showed off. The calm methodical bulldog approach of finding answers was the key to his success and much like the skills of a good negotiator. Unlike the capable high tech forensic TV detectives of today, Colombo was a personal train wreck. You could not stop watching his apparent ineptitude.

Tipping your hat to how capable you are might get others working harder to beat you. Keep your ego under lock and key. Save your knowledge and preparation for the right time and don't put everything on the table right away.

You Can't Argue with a Blank Wall

Look beyond negotiating positions or standpoints. When you discover the interest of others, you may find compromise and resolve issues. Getting someone off a position is very hard unless you know why he or she has that position. In negotiations, most people don't ask an important question.

Why are others asking for what they want? When you discover *why* people are asking for what they want, you may be able to find resolutions that will work for both sides. A position or demand can be a blank wall. You can't argue with it. Find out what's *behind* the wall. Listen intently until you discover why the other party is at the table.

Insight will make the difference and people skills will most likely be your strongest asset in negotiating. Everyone has different personality styles and traits. Determine how your behavior impacts others and adjust your style and behavior accordingly. Communication success is how well you relate and interface with others.

It's fairly simple to understand others' behavior and personality styles as long as you don't try to over think and play psychoanalyst. People are far too complex to figure out in a short period of time.

Think of painting the walls in a house with a wide paint roller, you're not using a fine artists paintbrush on a canvas. You're just trying to get an overview of people you're dealing with and their personality traits so you can better deal with them and the issues. Almost everyone will fit into one of four dominant styles:

Four Common Behavior and Personality Styles:

The Controlling Style, aggressive, dominant, get it done now, "it's my way or the highway"

The Reserved Style, steady, methodical, team player

The Talkative Style, influencing, tries to motivate others, wants you to like them

The Introverted Style, cautious, conscientious, detail oriented, "show me how" attitude

People may change their dominant style or use a combination of styles to accommodate a situation, be patient. In time people's personalities tend to show through, especially under stress. Have this thought in mind when you talk to people: what kind of communicators are they and what kind of personalities or styles do they have? Look for the style and adjust to it, but don't over think it and don't make it obvious.

You can't change what you are and people may see through you if you try. However, you can subtly *adjust* your style and that is all it takes to be effective. You are trying to get the piano in tune so it will play better. You don't want personality styles and friction blocking the negotiating process.

Adjusting to Different Styles:

Aggressive Personalities: they want fast answers and no flowers. Get to the point quickly, no chit chats.

Talkative and People Oriented: be friendly and social but do not underestimate them, they may be trying to sell you to their positions.

Good Listeners: be calm and steady as they are reserved. Slow down and control enthusiasm.

Introverted and Sticklers for Detail: be factual and specific. Everything you say may be challenged. Choose your words and details carefully.

The Power Tool

Be an Active Listener.

You learn real interests of others when you are an active and intent listener. It's never the story; it's always the emotion. Tone of voice and body language are the real keys to understanding communication. Be alert, listen intently, and watch closely.

When you're the active listener, others are doing the talking. They can talk themselves into a corner. Talk less and listen more, you'll be less likely to make mistakes. Let the other party make the mistakes for you.

> **Never Interrupt Others When They are Making Mistakes.**

You could fill thousands of pages of ideas on what to do, or just as important what not to do when negotiating. Negotiations are subjective and a process. Keep it simple, focused, and use common sense. Your people skills and the ability to read others will be your strongest assets.

Keys Negotiating Points:

Know what you want. What will be the best outcome for you? Know why this is important to you.

Find out what the other side wants as soon as possible. The other side would not be there if they had nothing to gain. What are they after?

Your power is your walk-away alternative. You never disclose this. If the deal or the situation is not possible, what is your next best choice? At what point will you walk away.

Do not allow authority or status to intimidate you. Your point of view or issues are not less important because you are dealing with powerful people.

If you are in a powerful position, do not let it go to your head. Remember how Colombo won. Keep your ego in check.

Be suspicious of deadlines. They may be phony and a ploy to pressure others into making bad decisions if time runs out. Challenge unfavorable timetables.

Listen intently. This is your most important skill. If you know you have a problem listening (and you know who you are) practice before negotiating. Make *active listening* your biggest asset.

People are poor listeners. Be sure you are getting your ideas across.

Be reasonable and flexible. Look for a satisfying agreement for both parties.

Negotiation is a process not an event. Remember the frog in the bowl of cream. Exhaust every opportunity to win or resolve the issues.

Deal honestly and ethically. Deal with integrity; you may need future opportunities to negotiate.

Leave something on the table. If you are ever planning to do business with someone again, remember negotiating is not poker where winner takes all.

Put it in writing. Write a note of understanding immediately what has been agreed.

Salary Negotiations? Yes, they are Different

Ground rules are different when negotiating salaries. For one thing, you don't have the ability to walk out if your boss turns down your request. However, if it's the last straw and you don't care about the outcome, it's a strong card to play. "Give me the raise I deserve or I quit," might work. However, have your desk cleaned out and be prepared to be shown the door.

In most situations, salary negotiations are a process you want to keep alive and ongoing. Companies *will* negotiate if you offer value; do not be afraid to negotiate. Your boss will be unlikely to approach you but don't be offended by that. It's up to you to state your position and take care of your needs.

How to Get That Raise:

Your current salary or what you made on your last job is not a factor under the following conditions: if you went to school and earned new credentials, learned a new skill, added a new responsibility, added more value, or did more work. This changes the game. Any time this happens is a good time to try to negotiate a raise. Go see your boss.

Never ask for a raise because you need one. Don't bounce into the bosses' office and ask for a raise without merit. Who cares what you need. Ask for a raise because you're an asset and bring benefits to the company. Never ask for a raise without a strong reason.

Negotiating a raise will likely be a process. Be prepared to think of it as ongoing. If you don't win the first round, start preparing for round number two as soon as you leave the office.

Set a time for discussions; select a meeting place where others will not interrupt you. Don't talk to your boss in an open casual atmosphere or you might not be taken seriously.

Be positive, upbeat and pleasant. Be strong. People will respect your efforts if you do it properly.

Don't let getting a raise be the topic of conversation in the office. It's your business alone.

Successful companies want and need good people to stay working, employee turnover is expensive and disruptive. Demonstrate your value and worth to the job and company. Put yourself in a stronger position to get a raise and you make it easier for yourself *and* your boss.

Want More Income? Forget Playing it Safe!

While you're busy thinking about how to earn more for yourself, are you thinking about what will earn more for your company? The secret to earning more income for yourself is not what you need or want, it's adding more value and profits. When you think income, do not negotiate solely on salary.

The more safety you demand, the more it's going to cost you. That's the price to pay for getting that steady paycheck. When you insist on security and demand your income solely as salary, you are saying regardless of your performance, you want your salary to remain the same. However, your company and your boss is likely thinking, you are not assuming any risk, so you will not likely share in any rewards.

Why?

Because you have tied yourself to an expense and you're a liability on the balance sheet, not as asset.

But if you say, "I am willing to take less salary but I want part of what I (or we) can produce," you have changed the negotiating game. You are now negotiating for the ability to earn more based on your performance. You're betting on yourself.

A KOOL Opportunity

When I started working at KOOL FM in Phoenix, the resources were limited and closely watched. The radio station was in a form of bankruptcy. As the company had no profits, it needed funding. The potential to improve sales and profits was among other things, to force our competitor out of format and prove to the financial partners that the station was capable of being a profit center.

I knew my negotiating position was not strong in this situation. Paying me a high salary would have put the company at a disadvantage regardless of my experience or value. The company needed to keep expenses low until it could generate profits. However, the station not having profits was an opportunity, but I had to assume the risk.

It was easy for everyone to focus negotiations on a percentage of profits that did not exist. I would not earn a penny more than my salary if I could not create profits; my incentive was based on performance. A smaller salary allowed me to negotiate a longer agreement and potentially I could earn much more if the station became successful. My income was tied to profits and that was far better than an annual contract that could be scrutinized and re-negotiated.

As I started out with this new company, I tightened my belt and living expense. I focused on the big picture and worked relentlessly on ratings and sales to improve the station.

As the station grew, our competitor changed format and the ratings and sales started uphill. KOOL went from last to first in the key demographic ratings of adults 25-54. It took four years for KOOL to become the leader in Phoenix radio. As sales soared, I was earning additional income on the profits. The investors and company could hardly be upset with the size of my income as the earnings were far exceeding the goals. I was an asset, not a liability.

I did not have to ask what I was going to earn for the next year, I just had to work on performance of the company. I was earning more and more income on the increasing profits and paid along with the owners. I was rewarded for the risk it took.

Deals are Done in the Beginning

An important lesson to be learned in salary and incentive negotiations is the best deals are made in the beginning, not the end. The more risk you assume in the beginning, the more you make at the end if things go well. When companies are new and cash and profits are tight, that's the time to take the risk. It's far easier to negotiate a piece of the future that doesn't exist than it is to demand a big salary.

When I was a salesman at WLYF in Miami, I was paid strictly on commissions. I was one of the first salesmen at the station and sales were just getting started. As the station became successful, I enjoyed the success and growth as well.

When the station became successful, my percentage of sales had grown even greater. I was producing almost 40% of the revenue of the entire radio station. Suddenly, I found my income had a spotlight on it. I was earning far more than the average radio salesman. I knew something was up.

"Would you like to be the Sales Manager," the company said.

"How does that work?" I asked.

"A steady salary," they said.

My ears perked up like a Doberman Pinscher.

The salary was generous and sure, it would be steady. But it was far less than the commissions I was earning over time. The logic was I would not have to worry about commissions if sales went flat. But I thought earning commissions with no salary *was* my security. As long as my value was what I produced, the more I sold the more secure I became.

"Thanks but no thanks," I said. "If you want to call me a sales manager, I'll take the title. But I want to make my money earning commissions."

As time went on, I made more than sales managers and even general managers. I felt even more security. I knew my name never came up as an overhead or expense; it was always tied to commissions and commissions meant profits.

So what I if I earned good income, it wasn't a salary. Later, as I went on to become a general manager, it took years to earn as much as I had as a salesman.

Are you willing to take the risk to get the reward? If you're confident you can produce more, think out of the box and get creative. Negotiate and bet on your performance and your ability to add value and make a difference. Putting your salary on the line speaks volumes. Bet on yourself and dare to be different otherwise your income will likely be average.

When negotiating, consider salary an expense to the organization. Try to tie yourself to productivity, sales, income or profits and you may be able to go from an expense to an asset.

Size of a Paycheck has little to do with Security

Someone earning fifty thousand a year may be an overpaid target while another earning six hundred thousand a year may be considered indispensable. To earn more income, be willing to think more like an entrepreneur. Add value, assume more risks and bet on yourself if you're in a position to do that.

Negotiating: A Manager's Tool

Enlightened workers will not respond to a hierarchical style of authority. Negotiating will be the tool of choice as leadership styles change to fit new times. In order for companies to hold on to the best people and stay competitive, they need to keep workers motivated and stimulated. It will take creative and innovative thinking. The work environment must accommodate individuals as well as teams. Managers need to be flexible and learn skills of good negotiators. It will likely be the best way to keep good workers from moving on.

Workers need good negotiating skills to achieve their goals. Being a good negotiator can mean a more satisfying role in your company as well as your personal life. To get the most from your efforts you must negotiate your needs and demands.

Steps to Success

- **The Will To Win Is To Prepare**
- **You Get What You Negotiate, *Not What You Deserve***
- **Lawyers Litigate, Everyone Else Negotiates**
- **Strong People Skills Are The Secret To Winning Negotiations**
- **Experienced Negotiators are the Active Listeners, Not Fastest Talkers**

Chapter 4

Relationships- Building Your Team

To be trusted is a greater compliment than to be loved
—**George MacDonald** (1824-1905)

We're in the Tank

It was June in 1983. My family and I got off the plane in Washington DC; it was a long flight from Honolulu. We walked outside to the open air and almost melted from the humidity. We had forgotten what east coast weather can be like in the summer.

I was the new manager of Viacom's radio station in Washington, WMZQ FM. My boss was Norman Feuer and president of the radio group. This was the second time I worked for Norm. He was my manager at WYLF FM in Miami years earlier.

"Welcome to Washington, business is in the tank and you're in the red. Go fix it." Norm had a great sense of humor.

"Thanks for the welcome," I said.

WMZQ was in a dogfight with 106 KIX Country. The stations had been battling for years and KIX was usually the winner. WMZQ sales were slow and off target, expenses were out of line and the ratings needed to be improved.

I focused on the big picture: advertising dollars chase the rating points. Improved ratings would fix any sales problems in short order. However, as long as Washington had two country stations splitting the audience, neither station was going to be a big winner.

WMZQ had done little research while KIX had a top-notch research company to help them with the music and the image of the station. KIX was able to zero in on the WMZQ weakness and ran "We play more music" TV commercials to position WMZQ as if it talked too much and did not play a lot of music.

I would have done the same thing if I were in their position. Our competition was using hardball tactics to force us out of the country format. Bob Cole was the KIX program director. He was young but he was a strong competitor and his station was in the lead. It's going to take talent and resources to win this battle, I thought.

I called a staff meeting and listened closely to how the competition was "cleaning our clocks." Not one person in the meeting had positive thing to say about our station, all the talk was about the competition.

After the meeting, I told everyone thanks for sharing the information. I said, from this day forward, I wanted to know what *we* were doing. Stop worrying and start planning I told everyone.

WMZQ had a huge news department that would have made a full time news station proud, it was dramatically overstaffed. The reality was, only one newsperson in morning drive needed to handle the news. Cutting the news commitment to a small staff would mean more music played and a big expense lifted.

I had little choice but to let the entire news department go. Word got around the market quickly. The new general manager is an, "Axe murderer in a hula skirt!"

Our program director had resigned. I called Bill Figenshu or "Fig" as we called him. He was our national program director working out of New York. Together we went on a nationwide search to find program director that would be up for this battle. We were at a convention in San Francisco when we realized, our best bet was back in Washington D.C. We recruited Bob Cole away from KIX. It was an offensive and defensive move. Our timing was impeccable.

KIX management was about turn up the heat on WMZQ and hire Gary D, an outspoken morning personality from a successful Cleveland radio station. This was a bold but risky move. An outrageous morning man could change the image of KIX from a "more music" station to a "more talk" station as the music image of KIX was the strength. Bob later told me one of the reasons he decided to join WMZQ was that should Viacom decide to take out the big checkbook, KIX would be in big trouble. A marketing battle between the stations would level the playing field and the easy win for KIX would be over.

Bob introduced us to Jim London the KIX morning talent. Jim decided to join WMZQ. We now have the KIX program director and morning man and KIX is about to risk it all with the Gary D. wildcard.

We had thrown gas on the fire. It was officially war. The press was having a field day with all the changes and that was good for business. We had more news coverage on WMZQ in one month than past years combined. Moral at the station improved, WMZQ was on the offense.

Find Good Partners

I met and hired E. Karl. I followed his radio consulting success across the country for years. His programming, research, and strategy skills were a perfect match for our situation. E. told me about a small boutique research company from San Diego specializing in radio programming and music. They also had extensive country music experience working with a similar station to WMZQ. Bob Harper came from San Diego for a meeting and I hired him to handle our music and strategy research.

These were big moves. We were putting a team together to fine-tune the station. The goal was to find weaknesses in our competitor and design and plan an offense strategy for WMZQ.

Harper told me about a new boutique production company specializing in TV commercials to promote radio stations working out of Nashville. I called Film House and talked to Curt Hahn. "Send me the demo reel of TV commercials that you've done to promote radio stations," I asked.

The demo TV commercial arrived the next day. And there it was, our ace in the hole. I was dancing around the office like a 5 year old. The commercial was as good as Wendy's "Where's the Beef?" or the Ernest P. Worrell "Hey Vern!" ads.

The Film House commercial had a funny looking guy with a big nose taking a shower with soap in his hair. He was lip-syncing the country hit, "It's Hard to Be Humble." People laughed aloud when they saw the commercial. I could not imagine a more positive music image that screamed, "Its fun to listen to country music." This commercial would be hard to forget and it had the potential to change the image of WMZQ. I called in our staff to get their reaction. "Ohhhh yes, we need this," was the reaction.

We tested the sing-a-long TV commercials in focus groups. People applauded and asked to see the commercials run again. The reaction was the same in every group we tested. The commercials were hilarious. I called Curt the next morning and told him what happened. "Start coming up with more ideas, we need more commercials," I said. Curt asked if he could come to our research studies to see how people reacted. That is a great idea I thought. The more Curt knows about our audience, the better we could design our TV commercials.

Think Big

"Brian, you're going to make a presentation to the Viacom executives in New York." This was the annual event for the radio general managers to stand court and present the business strategy and outlook for the coming year. My only experience to that point was with a small company and the owners were really entrepreneurs. My boardroom experience was lunch at McDonald's with fries, a shake and a walk on the beach.

I waited in the reception room with the other radio managers. I was not picking up ideas from anyone on what to expect. I would have to learn on the fly, I thought.

My turn came to present WMZQ. I walked in the room and thought I was on a Hollywood movie set.

"Oh My God," I said to myself.

The room filled wall to wall with corporate people. At the table were the Viacom executives, the accountants lined up against the wall on both sides of the long room. I started by telling the story of our aggressive competition.

"We're at war in Washington. If we do not take the lead, they will not stop. We will be dead in the water and WMZQ is going nowhere," I said. You could hear a pin drop. No one said a word.

CEO of Viacom Terry Elks was at the other end of what seemed like a mile long table. He casually raised his hand and said, "Brian, tell us what you're thinking."

I explained the plan. "We need to carpet-bomb our competitors out of existence," I said. "We need a massive concentrated TV campaign. We need to turn the tables on the competition and this is going take real money."

"We will go nowhere in the ratings if we don't do this. We need KIX out of the country format to get more shares of country audience from the marketplace." I again reminded everyone that WMZQ was a punching bag for the competition and had never made a real marketing presence in Washington.

"My plan is less expensive than continuing to lose money every year," I said. Terry asked a few more questions and seemed to like the ideas. No one else in the room said a word, only the two of us were talking.

I left the meeting feeling better than if I had soft peddled the problems. I was asking for a real TV marketing budget and knew I had to fight for it.

The station budget was approved; aggressive marketing for the station began. The programming had improved and quality of music was helping the sound of the station. E. was helping Bob with strategy and format ideas. Our sales effort was getting a boost from the talk on the street.

Some of the Washington Redskin "Hogs" were country music fans and agreed to call the station during morning drive and give us "Hog Reports" reporting happened the night before. We created a contest and played "Truth or Hogwash," the audience reaction was excellent. The image of the station kept improving.

Our competition was going the other way. The Business Review reported KIX morning man, "Gary D.'s provocative references to Mayor Marion Berry's wife's light complexion and the District of Columbia's high alien population," ran on the KIX morning show. The Washington Times ran a special two-part pullout section, "Country Music Battle on Air Heats Up." Radio and Records ran articles on, "The Battle for the Capital." Listeners were calling the station to tell us, "Those

KIX guys have killed their station, WMZQ sounds better than ever."

WMZQ ratings were climbing and our competitor felt the heat. Rumors began that KIX was going to change format. WMZQ was about to have the country radio format to itself, sales continued to improve on the news. We had put together a team of superstar resources and formed strong relationships. The best programming, research and marketing we could find was at our station.

I had just gotten back from the Bahamas celebrating with our sales force when Norm called. It was very early in the morning. Something was up I thought.

"I quit," Norm said.

"I'm leaving the end of the year and I'm moving back to San Diego. You're on the short list considered for the President's job."

No one had a clue this was going to happen. I was stunned. I called Fig. He was wired into the corporate rumors. I said what do you think and he said, "Go for it."

I did. It took months to get through the process but I was named President of Viacom Radio. We bought a house in New Canaan, Connecticut and I was back to working in New York City.

Trust Your Instincts

Norm had convinced Viacom to change the format of our station in New York City from a country format to easy listening music. They called it, WLTW, Lite FM. The programming was similar to the strategies used at WLYF FM in Miami years earlier only the music was brighter and played more vocals.

This was déjà vu, I had years of successful experience working this kind of radio format. I was confident this programming would eventually be a big winner in New York radio. Nevertheless, I was concerned about the marketing of the station and laser focused on the opportunity.

I met with the general manager of WLTW and knew this meeting was going to be difficult. George had competed hard to get the radio President's job. He was upset he did not get the position. He made no bones about not liking the situation nor did he want to report to me. I was too young and new to the company.

I thought at best, my relationship with George would be cordial. However, I needed his help to make the right moves work. George was a strong sales talent, a good fit for the station and had fierce loyalty from his staff. A real asset I did not want to lose. I asked George what he thought of WLTW and how it was going.

"It's doing great," said George.

"Yes it is, were off to a good start. But we're not on the radar screen and a lot of people in New York don't know about us," I said. We discussed programming and marketing ideas. George told me about the great TV campaign that was running.

"Let's see the commercials," I said.

We went into the conference room to see the TV commercials. I saw a problem immediately. The commercials were creative. They were too creative! The message of WLTW was lost in all the creativity. I could not remember seeing the dial position of the station and was not sure what they were saying about the new radio format or why I should listen to the station.

"We're lucky to have this creativity," George told me and everyone paid a retainer to have a "hot" ad agency like this.

Later in the day, I called George and asked him to come to my office.

"George, please get on a plane and go meet the people at Film House in Nashville. We do not pay retainers for ad agencies more than we pay our program directors. And the ad agency you're working with, while creative, has no concept of how the radio business works or what our needs are. I want you to work with people that have experience and understand how our business and ratings work. This will the station get to where we both know it can go."

Time was short. Our job was getting rating points and selling advertising. I knew more ad dollars would follow immediately if we marketed the station better and improved the ratings. We needed the flagship station in New York to be our sales leader if our radio group was to be successful.

George was a good sport and went along with my idea. I told George before you can win the game you need good resources. Try it my way and we will see what happens. If I am wrong, well look at other options. I told him I wanted him to stay at the job and lead the station.

Fig and I set out a strategic plan for the radio group. We hired E. Karl, Bob Harper and Film House to work with the stations in all of our markets; I was counting on the strategic relationships we had built at WMZQ in Washington.

Everything started to work; we had a group strategy in motion for all of our markets. All of the Viacom Radio stations in the group had the best research, the best consultants and the best marketing that we could find. And it made all the difference.

Sales quickly followed the ratings success and every station in our group was a leader in its format. George was having great success with WLTW and became a big supporter of our resources. I had won a cordial relationship with him.

The radio group had become a "Cash Cow" and advertising dollars were flying.

People Are the Business

I used an important principle to help create success. People are not just important to business. *People are the business.*

Relationships and friendships are at the heart of business and careers and a sure way to create success.

You must have good players at your side. Working together towards a common goal creates synergy. Relationships for mutual benefit are not about who you are, it's about what you do together. Synergy is a business advantage that's hard to beat; synergy is more powerful than the sum of the parts. The secret is to find relationships you can collaborate with and create more than you can on your own.

Companies move fast today and take advantage of changing environments. They have less reluctance to make moves. When survival or a critical advantage is on the line, things happen quickly. Competition, like adrenalin, speeds everything up. You have to run faster just to stay in place. Your personal safety net in times of change is your relationships. Fast moving times make networking and relationships more important than ever.

The work place used to be more stable. Relationships between customers and suppliers used to change slowly, workers stayed with the same company for generations and people made long-term commitments. But as the economy and businesses change, you too, must change your approach.

White-collar jobs are beginning to look more like jobs in the building and construction industry. People are moving from opportunity to opportunity. As jobs become more portable, your transferable skills will create opportunities for you.

Look to improve what is ahead of you; do not focus solely on what worked before. Relationships and networking have to be both inside and outside your workplace. If contractors and consultants have replaced jobs in your company, meet and include these new people in your relationships and networking. They may provide valuable help and insight for your career. The more things change, the more you have to rely on your own resources to create and cultivate a network.

How important is this? Very! The majority of new jobs and new opportunities will continue to come from who you know, not what you know.

Are People Reacting to Me?

In the workplace, we might not have the option of choosing who we work with. We will meet people we don't like and we will meet people that don't like us. When people have diametrically opposing personalities, very different viewpoints and little in common, there is not much to like. The best you can do is look to find common ground and make the best of it. Before you write off others because they don't like you, could you be the cause of the problem?

People have an intuitive sense about others and their attitudes. Communicating is not just what you say, its body language and how you say things. If you are sending signals, people will sense them. People who don't like you could simply be reacting to the communication you are sending.

Anyone not liking what they are doing is not likely to be happy. It's hard to hide that. Unhappy people may create problems for themselves faster than anyone else can. Self-criticism is like having a two by four board on your shoulder. Every time you turn, you're hitting someone with your attitude.

If your career is stopped or going nowhere, before you blame the economy or your company, stop and think. Could the greatest problem and your biggest enemy be in the mirror? If you can't stand yourself, it's doubtful anyone else will either.

Don't Take Yourself Seriously

If you don't like what you do, you could be showing it to everyone. If you lack confidence or have low self-esteem, it's unspoken. But those around you will sense it. If this is you, you need to cut yourself some slack. Until you get over yourself, relationships are going to be difficult to start or maintain. And if you can't build relationships, your career is going to suffer.

Stop taking yourself *so serious* and take people around you *more seriously*. Leaders and successful people have confidence and self-esteem. The more secure and successful people are, the more likely they are to make fun of themselves *But they rarely make fun of others.*

The paradox for low self-esteem and confidence is not taking yourself seriously. *Humor and humility are part of strong character.* Strong, secure people have tremendous affinity for others, and that makes them attractive. The more you like yourself, the more others will like you. Good relationships will start with you.

Relationships are Built on a Strong Foundation
- **Trust**
- **Commitment**
- **Honesty and ethics**
- **Mutual advantage and collaboration**

People form personal and business relationships for mutual advantage. As long as the advantage for both parties remains, relationships continue. However, relationships need a strong foundation to hold them together for any length of time. Without trust, commitment, honesty and ethics, no matter what the reason a relationship was formed, it might not last.

Trust is Having Each Other's Best Interest in Mind
Trust is a key element in a relationship. When you make commitments to others, it is no longer, "Every man for himself." Relationships are founded on mutual interest. You consider the interest of others as well as yourself. If this trust is broken, you will no longer have trusted partners. In order for

people to be open and collaborative with new thoughts and creativity, you must have trust. Trust is agreeing that each party has the others' best interest at heart. Like the gunfighters in the old west movies, "You're covered, I've got your back," is what relationships and friendships are built on.

You must be able to trust others in order to share your important ideas. Integrity is everything.

Spine and Resolve

"On s'engage et puis on voit!" said Napoleon Bonaparte which means, "One jumps into the fray, then figures out what to do next." When you have relationships with strong commitment, your spine and resolve will support others. Committed relationships last through problems, adversity, disappointments, arguments and bumpy roads.

Commitment separates the players from the talkers; commitment is the ingredient of successful people. It means you will take action and you can be counted on to do what you say. No excuses; you're in the game and you're not leaving until the game is over. It's a sign of strength and courage.

Honesty and Ethics

"Always do right. This will gratify some and astonish the rest," said Mark Twain.

Even among thieves, honesty prevails. These concepts are so important they allow people that don't particularly like each other to have strong long lasting relationships. Many people don't consider honesty and ethics to be critically important. That is, however, until it affects them directly. As soon as you are in a relationship where you are counting on others, you will appreciate ethical and honest behavior.

Ethics are the rules and standards governing the conduct of a person. Simply, you don't want to work with jerks who can't tell right from wrong or don't care. If you allow that to happen, sooner or later, you will be directly affected by someone's lack of ethics. Choose carefully the people you want to have relationships with. If people work without honesty and ethics, it's only a matter of time until you are personally and negatively involved. People will judge you by the way you handle your relationships with others.

Mutual Advantage and Collaboration

Motivation is the essence of relationships and while people do things for their own reasons, relationships are formed *for mutual gain*. In business, nothing is stronger than the synergy of working together for mutual advantage. The interaction of people creates a very strong force. If you have no partners to work with, it may be hard to develop ideas to the fullest.

A Strong Personality May Hear No Reason

One principle occurs over and over again. A strength overused *may become your biggest weakness*. Your character strength, which can be your biggest asset, can be your demise if you have a closed mind. When you work with others, people bring a new perspective as they can see things differently. People with different interests often get to the same goal, but from different directions. Collectively, you gain strength that will help you overcome problems and obstacles. Be open and receptive to new ways of thinking; respect others for their ideas.

Surviving the Subarctic

I worked with Human Synergistics® Survival Simulations and watched people create synergy. People working together can develop solutions that are superior to those working on an individual basis. As part of the Subarctic Survival Situation™, developed by J. Clayton Lafferty and copyrighted by Human

Synergistics (Plymouth, MI: 1973, 2005), participants individually tried to figure out how to survive after their floatplane crashed in a remote area near the Quebec-Newfoundland border. The pilot was killed and unable to contact anyone before the crash. Everyone who survived had warm clothes, but no one to guide them to safety. The time of year was October. Every day the weather was getting worse and the ice-cold winter was setting in.

The survival exercise is to rank 15 items salvaged from the plane. They are to be ranked in order of importance to survival. The salvaged items included a fifth of rum, a hand axe, a magnetic compass and a safety razor shaving kit with a mirror. In order to determine what was critical for survival, participants had to take into consideration factors including weather, food, and warmth and how they were going to get to safety.

Everyone reviewed the situation by themselves. They independently ranked the items in order of importance for survival. People were not allowed to discuss their answers with anyone.

After they finished their individual rankings, the participants formed small groups of five to seven people. In these small groups, they discussed the same situation but now it was discussed as a team. They exchanged ideas and expressed their viewpoints. They had to come to a group consensus and agree on what were most important items for survival.

When the exercise was finished, the experts' correct rankings were presented. Everyone could now see how they had scored. Each of participants had calculated an individual score and everyone was part of a small team.

In almost every case, people ranking the items independently made the wrong selections. What individuals considered most important for their survival was wrong. They did not survive.

And virtually every group that worked together with a consensus solution picked the right items and the group of people survived.

Collaboration produced the right answers. Listening and exchanging ideas is a catalyst for different viewpoints and solutions. People thinking and working together many times will see problems and opportunities that individuals miss.

Bill Gates, the richest man in the world, is quoted as saying without Paul Allen and Steve Ballmer, there would be no Microsoft. Why? Look at the different personalities working together you see Microsoft is a synergy of skills, not one person's idea. Bill needed others with skills he did not have. Together, they formed the synergy to create success.

This is a hard lesson for people of strong character that want to be independent and work alone. People may work alone but they will likely be limited. When we study history, we find examples of strong individuals and solitary leaders. But most often, the strong support is not mentioned in the press or writings of great people. Thomas Jefferson, Winston Churchill and Warren Buffet are studied as individuals, but they had great support as well. One person can only do so much. Many skills are needed to accomplish big goals. Behind successful people, you will find great support, relationships and synergy.

Find a Horse to Ride

Lifetime employment is no longer a fact of life and you'll likely have many jobs and even multiple careers. For some, a career as a leader or manager is not what is wanted or needed. You may let others lead the way to success, you do not have to be the one to change the world or unleash the power within. If you hitch your wagon to a rising star, it can lift you to new heights.

Set your sights and goals on finding the next Google, Microsoft or talented entrepreneur who needs your help. Build your relationships around winners and look for companies and individuals you have confidence in. Find the best horse to ride until it falls down. The go-go attitude, "I can do it by myself," strategy sells books. However, it is not what will work for the majority of people. Use your assets to their full potential when supporting others. Get on the right team at the right time and you may be able to climb the ladder of success.

You are the judge of your abilities and knowing what you want to do with your career. Being a supporter in a winning situation may be just as rewarding as winning alone. Focus on what you want to do and do not settle for less. You are most productive when you enjoy what you are doing. You cannot support others or develop good relationships if you are not happy. You do not have to do it alone, work on improving relationships with winners and the successful.

Companies and Relationships

We are at the beginning of a new age and a new way of doing business. We are dealing with smarter competitors. Individuals, entrepreneurs and start-ups use relationships in a synergetic way to build a better business model. Companies that use the old hierarchical style of organization and management will have the problems of higher turnover. If companies expect to get the best from workers, they need to be thinking how to develop and maintain long-term relationships.

Companies need talented and motivated people to remain competitive. Without good relationships, it is almost impossible to create synergy. Workers that do not feel they have a good place to work will just commit to putting in time and little else. In the end, companies would be better off investing and helping their own people instead of looking outside. Long-term relationships are good for business.

Motivation is a Skill?

Motivation is a misunderstood opportunity. However, if you catch on to the secrets, you will be able to lead and help others more effectively. The next chapter may change your perspective on how you deal with people.

Steps to Success

- **Trust, Honesty And Ethics Will Count The Most, *When You Need It The Most***
- **Recruit The Best Players To Your Team**
- **Lasting Relationships Are About Advantage And Collaboration**
- **Expand Your Personal Network**
- **A Working Relationship *Is* Synergy**

Chapter 5

Motivation-Marching to Your Own Drum

Motivation is the art of getting people to do what you want them to do because they want to do it.
—Dwight David Eisenhower
34th President of the United State

We understand motivation because it drives all of us. But do we understand why we can't drive other peoples' motivations? Personal motivation is a one-way mirror you stand behind, it lets you see out. Others trying to look in only see a reflection of themselves and their motivation.

People are different. Everyone has unique backgrounds, viewpoints, cultures and experiences. People see things from *their perspective, not your perspective.* When you do not consider other people's points of view, attempts at motivation will likely fail or may be interpreted as manipulation.

To motivate people, create an environment that allows people to motivate themselves. Managers and human resource people are often on the wrong track only trying to fix problems. Long-term success comes from the natural strengths of individuals; the secret is to manage around weakness. People feeling they are contributing and getting recognition will likely be the most motivated.

Workers doing a job for their own reasons are more likely to be productive, have a better attitude and less reluctance. Workers that do not like what they are doing are more likely to be poor performers. While one worker feels enrolled, the other feels manipulated. One worker is motivated, and one is not.

> A man shows his greatness by the way he treats the little man. The value you place on people determines whether you are a motivator or a manipulator of men. Motivation is moving together for mutual advantage. Manipulation is the moving together for my advantage. That is a substantial difference. With the motivator everybody wins. With the manipulator only the manipulator wins. The win for the manipulator is temporary and the price is prohibitive.
> **—Thomas Carylyle**

People working at a job they do not enjoy see the paycheck as manipulation. It does not matter how hard you try to motivate them. If it were not for the paycheck, they would not be working. People who enjoy work feel better about themselves and have more self-esteem. To them, the paycheck is recognition of contribution, not manipulation.

Allow others to have their own reasons to be motivated. It's not a blow to the ego to have others see things differently and not agree with you. The goal of reaching a budget or achieving a performance level may be your reasons and are important to you. But is it important to others? That depends on what's in it for them. Enthusiasm for you is not enthusiasm for me, *unless we make it mine*. Working on creative and innovative ways for others to be motivated will help your cause.

The manager of APECO copy machines bought a house from my uncle Jerry. My uncle knew I needed a job and arranged an interview for me; I was hired on the spot. The job was fixing copy machines and doing minor repairs. I reported to work and was told, "When you go on service calls, try to sell customers a service agreement. We'll give you a list of old machines in the territory not in use. See if you find those customers or any others we don't know about. Fix the copiers, try to sell a service agreement and get orders for fresh copy paper. We'll pay you fifteen dollars commission for every service contract you sell."

My salary was only one hundred and fifteen dollars a week. I quickly figured selling a few agreements weekly would give me a 30 or 40% raise. I had no idea that other service people were only selling one or two agreements month. I was thinking I would sell one every other day or so. Little did I know what was expected of me.

Gold in the Old Factories

The territory they gave me was the old Ironbound industrial section of Newark, New Jersey. The neighborhood was poor and surrounded by old buildings and factories. Streets had potholes and railroad tracks ran everywhere. The company had not serviced the area for years. I guessed as young and inexperienced as I was, they would start me out where I could learn something and not do much harm. As it turned out, the territory was a gold mine for sales, a hidden gem. Copiers sold years ago were in those old buildings and factories.

In the days before Xerox and the plain paper copiers, you needed two sheets of paper and a chemical to make copies. You threw away the negative piece of paper after you made a copy. Almost all copy machines were designed to make 8 ½ by 11 or legal-size copies.

When I went into an office or factory, it was usually a surprise. I was so young many asked if I was still in high school. The account list the company gave me was out of date so I decided it was just as easy to go into every office and ask if they had an old copier around. When I was able to find an old copy machine and got it operating, I usually got an order for fresh copy paper. And many times, I sold a service agreement. But I was never sure if people were buying from me because they felt guilty after I fixed the machines for free or because I was so young, energetic and enthusiastic. Back at my office, I was off the radar screen and unsupervised. I just handed in the orders and went about my business.

One day, I was in an old building and saw an office with a small sign on the door. It said, "City of Newark Engineering." I went in and saw blueprints on big tables scattered everywhere. In the corner, I spotted an old APECO machine. It was a lot bigger than the letter size copiers; it could run large 11 x 17 copy paper. Dust on the cover told me this machine had not been used in years.

I took the cover off and found the copier was in perfect condition, it might never have been used. I put in fresh chemicals and asked if I could use a blueprint as a test. It made a great copy and everyone was surprised how good it was.

"How do you make copies of your blueprints and other things you need?" I asked the staff.

"Everything is sent to a blueprint service," they said.

I asked if they had need for quick copies. The answer in unison was yes, every day it seems we have emergencies. I told the staff I could special order large copy paper that would run in this old machine. They agreed that would help as they could copy critical sections of the blueprints and save time.

One Sale Can Change Everything

"Buy a service agreement and let me order paper for you. I can have this system running within two days," I said. They said start us with enough paper to make 5,000 11 x 17 copies.

I about fell over. To this point, I was selling customers 250 sheets of paper, and occasionally 500 sheets of letter size paper. But the size and cost of this order was huge. I went back to the office and ordered the paper. I found myself no longer the new, young, inexperienced technician. I had become one of the top servicemen in the New York region selling service agreements and copy paper. The next morning the manager of the office called me to his office.

"I want you to join our sales meeting and meet our senior sales people tomorrow morning," he said.

The meeting was early in the morning; we were all crowded together in the manager's office. The meeting started without introduction, the room got quiet.

Listen Harder, Sell More

The manager said that if you want to survive and do well in this tough business, you will learn that what you know about copy machines is not the most important thing.

"Unless you can sit in the seat of the person you are talking to, wear that person's clothes and shoes, see that vision from behind that desk, you cannot sell that person a thing," he continued.

"Your job is to find out what that person knows and sees. You can only sell people what they need, not what you want to sell. You don't sell a copy machine because you want to make a commission. People will buy copy machines because they need to. Your job is to find out what the needs are. Then you can sell them something. Talk less and ask questions, listen and learn. That's how you become a top salesman. You motivate people to do things when you understand how to help them. You sell more when you listen more and talk less."

I had no idea this was the way to sell things. I thought you talked a lot until you were able to sell something. I realized I was only doing well because of my youth and enthusiasm.

What the manager said made more and more sense. See things from the customers' point of view.

The meeting was over in no time, I wanted it to last longer and learn more. Everyone in the room seemed energized and ready to sell more copy machines. I thought to myself, I was going to sell even more paper and service contracts.

I used the selling tips I had just learned and found out selling was not talking more; it was more about listening and learning. My sales performance soared. I was promoted to a copy machine sales job, my sales career was off and running. By 24, I was in midtown New York City having changed jobs to join SCM Corporation. Part of my new job was training new sales people.

What I learned in that first sales meeting stayed with me in all my years of sales. The key is to understand others. Their motivation to buy, not my reasons to sell was critical. The more you know, the more you can sell.

My early experience of sales taught me lessons about motivation, although at the time, I had little understanding about how it worked. I saw the opportunities, became self-motivated and that carried me to success. No one in the office helped me until I *became* a success. But once I got recognition and acknowledgment, it motivated me even more.

The ability to be self-directed with little supervision was a big plus for me. The loosely managed environment allowed me to motivate myself and served my needs.

Desire is the Key to Motivation

Desire and motivation are the ultimate powers directing our actions and behavior. When we are motivated to do something, we get things done and we make things happen. Successful people and leaders want to surround themselves with motivated people as they have better attitudes and are more productive. Everywhere we hear about the importance of motivating others. It's no wonder we have countless workshops, seminars and books about motivation to help our business and ourselves.

When we get people together for meetings, pep talks and encouragement, we use excitement and enthusiasm and "stoke the fires" or "rally the troops."

But for people who are not self-motivated, the excitement of meetings and pep talks wears off quickly. Enthusiasm wanes. In reality, it is extremely rare you can make people do things and motivate them. A paycheck is big incentive but typically has little to do with motivation.

People do things out of necessity but real motivation comes from personal reasons. Motivation means different things to everyone. Money, power, sex, family happiness, job satisfaction, recognition, sports, independence or even something as simple as reading books to children motivate people.

But I Thought I was Motivating Others

I started a job managing a radio station and discovered a department head was having meetings 7:30 in the morning on a regular basis. The general offices opened at 8:30 AM. I asked workers in the department how they felt about the job and discovered many had a hardship getting to work so early. I asked if any of them had brought this up to the manager. They all replied, "Not a good idea." They said the manager was not approachable.

I asked the manager how he felt about the people in his department. He said everyone was motivated, everyone comes in early, and we get more done.

I said, that is certainly true, you do come in early. But you do have a morale problem. You are asking people to come in early. It appears you're doing this for your own reasons and to make it look like you are working harder. But productivity in your area is no higher than before you had early morning meetings. And you're taking advantage of workers for your benefit, not theirs. He said he thought he was doing the best for the company.

"With unhappy employees, how could you possibly expect more productivity?" I said.

Many times, people will put up with a bad situation rather than bring it to management. It is up to managers and leaders to ask how they can support people better. The first step in going from hierarchal management to leadership is developing a good ear. You cannot fix what you do not know. People that are not good listeners will never understand how to motivate others. The more you listen, the better your chances are to figure out how to motivate someone.

Do not get wrapped up in thinking you can talk people into having a positive attitude. That's not as important as you think. Help people become a positive force for themselves, that's important. People develop a positive attitude and self-esteem when they feel they are being productive. Listen for clues and people will tell you how to motivate them.

I learned the following motivating principles during my DiSC® Personal Profile System® leadership training. The courses in behavior help understand people and develop strong leadership skills.

Everyone has a unique mental DNA similar to everyone's uniquely different fingerprint. Accepting others for their differences helps you put these rules in practice and improves your management and leadership skills.

Motivational Principles:
- **You can't motivate other people**
- **All people are motivated**
- **People do things for their reasons, not your reasons**

- **A person's strength overused may become their weakness**
- **The very best one can do to motivate others is to create an environment that allows specific individuals to motivate themselves**

People understand motivation from their perspective; it is what works for them. However, you cannot assume your motivation will work for others. Those in authority misunderstanding this principle will have a difficult time in a leadership role.

The best way to motivate people is to create a better environment and change *your* attitude towards others. The principle is simple but not easy to accomplish. It takes a strong leader to let others do it their way.

Key Ideas to Motivate Others:

1. People are individuals. Respect different ways of thinking and doing things. Accepting the individuality of others is a sign of strength and leadership. Innovation and creativity thrive on self-expression.

2. People that choose their own goals and self-interests will perform the best.

3. People want to feel they are making a contribution, being heard, recognized and acknowledged.

4. People want to have their own skills improved and developed for their own personal reasons.

5. Hierarchal management styles are in conflict with motivation.

6. Do not overlook small important day-to-day things in favor of big splashy events.

7. Make it a habit to look for opportunities to praise people for their work and efforts.

8. Private and personal praise is important but public praise in meetings and in front of peers is monumentally rewarding and motivating.

9. Admit you wrong when you screw up and others will respect your integrity.

10. Don't tell others what to do, or how to do a job. Give them goals and leave the people alone.

11. Don't micromanage, it's demoralizing and debilitating and you will make workers feel like victims.

12. Keep people informed if you want them motivated.

The workforce today is brighter and more enlightened than ever and will respond to good leadership. The managers and leaders that listen to people and learn more about them will be the most effective. *Make accommodations for people if you expect to motivate them, do not try to make one size fit all.*

It is good business to think of people as unique individuals. They are the most important asset in any business or organization. Motivation drives performance, enhances careers, and creates better working environments that allow creativity and innovation.

A connected global economy will need more than technology and productivity to win. Keeping workers motivated may be the best answer to staying competitive.

Steps to Success

- **All People Are Motivated**
- **You Can't Motivate Others**
- **Understanding Motivation Becomes A Powerful People Skill**
- **People Do Things For Their Own Reasons, Not Yours**
- **Change The Environment And Let People Motivate Themselves**

Chapter 6

Persistence-
Thick Skin Required

Press on: nothing in the world can take the place of
perseverance. Talent will not; nothing is more common than
unsuccessful men with talent. Genius will not; un-rewarded
genius is almost a proverb. Education will not; the world is
full of educated derelicts. Persistence and determination
alone are omnipotent.

—Calvin Coolidge
30th President United States

Growing up in Brooklyn, New York, Lee Dunham dreamt
of being an entrepreneur. He had a shoeshine stand and
collected milk bottles while the other kids were out playing.
Lee came from a black family of laborers. He would tell his
mother, "When I grow up, I want to start my own business."
His mom told him time after time, "There's no way you're
going to open your own business."

Lee grew up, but never forgot his dream. He joined the Air
Force after high school, enrolled in the Air Force food service,
and promoted to officer's cook. After the Air Force, he worked
for restaurants including the Waldorf Astoria in New York
City. He went to night school to sharpen his business skills and

applied to the police academy. Lee started a fifteen-year full time career as a beat cop in Harlem's 28th Precinct.

Passion, Drive & Determination

His commitment to own a business never stopped. Lee continued his night classes and worked part time jobs. "I saved every penny I earned as a police officer. For ten years, I didn't spend one dime. No movies, no vacations, no trips to the ballpark." He had one focus, owning a restaurant.

He put restaurant business plans together but he could not get financed. The idea of a "classy tablecloth place" was not going to happen. "Not too many banks willing to lend a lot of money to a black guy in 1971," said Lee. But his dream did not fizzle out. He would find another way and thought about franchising. Lee tried Chicken Delight and others. Finally, he met with McDonald's and they agreed to a franchise but it had to be in the inner city.

Lee put his life savings of $42,000 on the line and borrowed another $150,000 to start the business. In 1971, Lee opened the first McDonald's franchise in Harlem, New York, a very tough neighborhood. Problems started right away.

No Turning Back

On opening day kids threw things at Ronald McDonald, they had to bring the clown back to the restaurant for safety. The crowd yelled, "You're not from the neighborhood. You're not a brother. Come back when you're black!" Things continued downhill after the store opened. Street gangs and gunfire scared customers away. Employees stole food, took the cash and robbed the safe. Lee had to hire his cop friends to keep the gangs out of the restaurant. His confidence was shaken but Lee was not going to quit so easily after years of sacrifice and commitment.

Lee understood poor black people. He knew what they were thinking and how hopeless they felt. He thought of a strategy, came up with a plan and called the gang members to a meeting.

"I grew up poor, just like all of you," Lee told them. "But I will not allow the restaurant to be a battleground any longer." He challenged them to stop the violence and fighting. It was time to rebuild their lives he said, and convinced the gang members they were only hurting themselves. He offered them jobs and agreed to train them to run a business but only if they worked at the restaurant.

"The only escape of being poor is to work your way out," Lee said. The gang members created goals, learned management skills, and street fighting in front of the restaurant stopped. The Harlem franchise went on to become one of the most profitable in the McDonald's chain earning over $1.5 million dollars a year. Lee was able to rebound and build a restaurant management business. Today he owns restaurants in New York and New Jersey and employees over 500 people.

The Essential Attributes

The majority of experienced and successful people agree passion, drive and determination are crucial for success. However, the persistence holds commitment together. If you are persistent enough, something will happen, it always does. The problem is you cannot choose the day, time or how long it takes to accomplish your goals. Things seem to happen on their own timetable.

Head winds and resistance along the way are part of the challenges. At times, it may seem like everything is working against you. Stress creates doubts and wears people out. Many throw in the towel too quickly just as they are on the verge of success. Staying the course is what determines the outcome, not how long it takes. If you persist long enough, you can win.

Courage Is Commitment and Doubt

It takes courage to make commitments but fear of failure may be in back of the mind. No one is immune from doubt. Overcome fears by focusing on goals and don't wimp out at the first sign of things not going your way. If needed, change the rules or adopt a new plan. Nothing is over until you quit.

Blue Book Directories

A friend told me about a job at Fairchild Publications Directories division in New York City. I was able to get an appointment with the advertising sales manager.

"How do people and companies use these books?" I asked. The ad manager told me buyers from stores and companies across the country come to New York City to buy merchandise. Thousands of men's, women's clothing and accessories manufacturers have offices in the New York area and the Blue Book directories list the address and phone numbers. Our advertising department sells ads in these books. We have five sales people selling and we have a list of accounts open now. "Are you interested in the job?"

I thought it would be a good way to learn the advertising and the fashion business. I was debating making this move when the ad manager continued.

"You would have a salary and earn commissions as you sell the ads. It should take a month or so to get your first order. If you do well selling Blue Books, I will help you get in line for an interview at one of our other publications."

This was an interesting carrot to dangle in front of me, but I was not looking years ahead, I was interested in making a successful move now. However, I thought his expectations were low. I could not imagine going a month and not making a sale. I took the job.

In my first week, I sold three ads. Later I found out it had been months since anyone had sold three new ads in a week. It appeared I was the only one making sales calls on new prospects. By the second week, I was clearly outselling everyone. One afternoon I received at note; all sales people are to attend a meeting early the next morning.

You're Fired!

The sales force gathered for the meeting.

"We are closing the Blue Book directories. The division is no longer able to make a profit and starting to lose money. We will finish selling ads in the last publication and that will be it, the department will be closed."

I'm on the job a few weeks and my advertising career is over. This must be a record, I thought. I decided as I can earn commissions until the division is closed, I'm going to focus on selling all I can to get a good letter of recommendation.

I came in early every day to get started; I was committed to go out in a blaze of glory. My sales continued to improve. But I felt like I was the only one trying to sell. Others in the sales staff looked like a herd of deer caught in the headlights of a car. They were all hanging around the office. Weeks rolled by, the cutoff date was at hand. The ad manager called everyone to his office, one at a time. I was the last one to be called.

The ad manager told me, "You've done a great job here; we want you to stay with the company. We have no job for you yet," he continued, "but we are going to find you one." For weeks, I sat at my desk and did nothing. I took long lunches and walks in Greenwich Village. Finally, my phone rang.

"Please come and meet Peter the ad director of Women's Wear Daily." I was offered a job.

I went home thinking, had I slacked off and not committed to improving my sales and getting a referral letter, this opportunity never would have happened. It would have been impossible to get a job like this, my age and inexperience would have worked against me. It pays to be focused and it sure pays to hustle I thought.

Focus on Important Stuff

Keeping a short-term focus can help things happen quicker. You don't want to lose sight of the long-term but you do not want to obsess over it either. Things can happen at a moments notice. Life and business can be spontaneously unpredictable and some of the best opportunities are not the things you are working on or create. Opportunities can come from what others do or from things that happen to you. Grab the opportunities as they come and fix problems as they appear. If you do not stay focused on the short term day-to-day, you might never get to your long-term goals. Focus on things you can control, work the on things within your grasp.

Develop a sense of priority and focus. Be careful not to get caught up in the minutia of day-to-day noise that can waste a lot of time.

Do not let other people and things distract you from your goals. Analysis by paralysis may stop you from moving ahead because things appear complicated. Work on keeping things as simple as necessary but no simpler. Successful people have the ability to cut through distractions and zero in on priorities.

Don't Mistake Movement for Achievement

Have a clear sense of what you want and be sure you are passionate and determined to follow through. If you are not totally committed, do not dabble with just average ideas. Pass them up. Like the game of baseball, people get a turn at bat. Pitches (opportunities, ideas, demands, and concepts) are thrown at you all the time. But not all pitches are worth swinging at. Wait for the good ones and don't feel obligated to swing at everything coming your way. Protect your integrity; say *no* when you are not fully committed. When you do make commitments, you will know you are ready and others around you will know the difference.

Even the most careful preparation will not prevent failure, things happen. Make dogged persistence a habit, it will keep you focused and you will keep trying. The more failures you have, the more learning experiences you get. Failures bring you closer to success, be prepared to get up and run at it again.

The carpenter tells students to measure twice, cut once. In business, the more you know the more money and time you can invest. Knowledge, insight and doing homework increase the odds of success. It is far easier to make a commitment when you have confidence.

> The stronger your fire, the greater your potential. Anyone can dabble, but once you've made that commitment, your blood has that particular thing in it, and it's very hard for people to stop you.
>
> **—Bill Cosby**

How many authors, actors and successful business people have become overnight successes? Not many. When you dig into details, you'll find many of the rising stars had been waiting tables and stringing tennis rackets for years before success. As we tend to focus on what we see, we can easily overlook the steady drive and struggle it takes to be a winner. Most leaders and successful people do not become overnight sensations. Quick success is an illusion.

One of the most successful and influential men of the century was Dale Carnegie. He wrote "How to Win Friends and Influence People" in 1936 and it became an unprecedented best seller. What's even more amazing, after an estimated fifteen million copies sold in thirty-eight languages and years later, it's still a best seller. "How to Win" is considered the father of the self-help movement. Yet few know how unsuccessful Carnegie's career was, until he became a published author.

Fabulous Failure

"The reason I wrote the book was because I have blundered so often myself that I began to study the subject for the good of my soul," said Dale. The story of his life is like a who's who on how to flop. He never finished college, he tried careers in just about everything including, selling, acting, writing, and even farming. It got so bad he became suicidal. But he rebounded and became determined to be successful. Ironically, his failures were fascinating to successful people. That's what made him a success.

After years of study and observations, Dale concluded it took determination, persistence and self-confidence to be a winner and that's where most people were lacking. He told people about his ideas and began teaching nonacademic courses to help others. At first people thought he was teaching public speaking. But as his teachings evolved, it became clear that he was trying to teach people to confront their fears and show them how to reach their potential. One of the great thoughts of the book is that you can make more friends by becoming interested in other people than trying to get other people interested in you. Dale was a success after years of failure because he never quit trying. His salvation was his persistence; he never gave up on himself. He realized his fear of failure could only be overcome if he confronted it.

Commitment, Persistence and Focus are not catchwords. They are ingrained in the thinking of the successful.

Success is the ability to go from one failure to another with no loss of enthusiasm.
                                                            —Winston Churchill

Thick Skin

Making commitments will invite obstacles. Problems will be the norm, not the exception. When you achieve success, everyone rallies to your side and suddenly, you were right all along. However, when you start on a path, it is usually on your own. You will need a thick skin to keep the doubters and negative influences out of your life. Think like the racehorse trainers that put blinders on horses to keep them from seeing side-to-side and getting distracted.

Everyone will want to jump in your boat when you're successful, but until that point, be prepared to row like crazy as others will just be watching. It takes guts to make real commitments and persistence to stay with a game plan. Develop a thick skin and stay focused. Don't let other people or things distract you from your goals.

> The starting point of all individual achievement is the adoption of a definite major purpose and a specific plan for attainment. Without persistence, you will be defeated before you start. With persistence, you will win.
> **—Napoleon Hill**
> Think and Grow Rich

Leaders and managers do it different, for different reasons. Read about common sense, horse sense and "Peters" principle of a nonsense strategy that happens all to often.

Steps to Success

- **Quick Success? It's An Illusion!**
- **Being Persistent Takes Courage**
- **A Thick Skin Helps Keep Negatives Out Of Your Life**
- **Failing Is Usually The First Step To Winning**
- **Don't Be So Quick To Quit, You Never Know What's Around The Corner**

Chapter 7

Leadership- Getting Others to Follow You

We have good corporals and good sergeants and some good lieutenants and captains, and those are far more important than good generals.

—William Tecumseh Sherman (1820-1891)

Are leaders born that way? Did they have to learn how to be leaders? It could be both, but it has little relevance because you can't tell the difference in performance. Leaders inspire with skills and charisma; they have unique styles but common traits. It's a way of thinking and acting. Their skills and personalities run the gamut. However, no single style is more effective than another.

Everyone sees leaders from their own perspective. The style that inspires you is what you're looking for, not what others value. Start with the ideal model in your head, one that works for you. Add your unique personality style as you master skills.

Most people don't want to become leaders but they do want success. Many enjoy independence and working alone while others don't want the extra responsibility. Some want to be part of a team and enjoy supporting roles. Regardless of your career, understanding skills and traits of leaders may give you a helpful perspective. Learn from the successful to improve yourself.

> As I grow older, I pay less attention to what men say. I just watch what they do.
>
> **—Andrew Carnegie**
> Industrialist

Managers and Leaders are Different

People often talk about management and leadership as if it's the same. It's not. The function is different.

Managers are in that position to supervise. They rely on operating skills, organizational ability and use power, authority and resources to achieve the organizational goals. The main concern is to be sure employees get things done right, and with efficiency. Managers solve problems and create policies. Managers at times may be leaders.

Leaders develop visions, use business insight and rely on communication and people skills. They empower others to get results. They ask more questions dealing with problems and uncertainty. They are the change makers in organizations and look for ways to do things better, even if it's different. The big challenge to leaders is recognizing and employing untapped ability and opportunities. Leaders at times may be managers.

Entrepreneurial organizations tend to have less formal arrangements of the decision making and supervision process.

Established companies tend to have layers of management and are more bureaucratic. The difference between leaders and managers is style and how they use different skills. Leaders have a high level of consistency as they say what they believe and do what they say. They deal directly and openly with problems. Leaders do what they think is right and are not afraid to get people angry when making an unpopular decision. Leaders are not in popularity contests.

Secrets of Exceptional Leaders:

Thick Skin and Courage

Like the pioneers in the old west, leaders are in front of the pack and often get mistaken for the enemy. They can get shot in the back. It takes courage to stay with a plan and vision that has not materialized. Critics don't wish them success; even friends and allies can develop weak knees in the thick of battle. Leaders don't lose sight of where they are going. They believe what they are doing is right and stay the course.

Priority

Leaders have vision and a sense of priority. It might be only two or three critical decisions a year to make a difference. They look for an edge and focus on the big picture. They filter out the day-to-day distractions and the "noise" of operations.

Horse Sense

Good judgment or sound sense, call it horse sense. Leaders use common sense thinking while others may be confused about having any common sense. Followers try to gain consensus and peer approval, as they don't want the risk of making mistakes. Academic and educated people may have bad judgment and common people can be brilliant leaders. Horse sense has little to do with intelligence or IQ; it's an intuitive skill developed from experience.

Active Listening Skills

Leaders are active listeners, they pay attention. They seek quality information and insight to make decisions and draw conclusions but not to gain consensus. Advice from people with real life successful experience is valued above all others as leaders seek accomplished people in their fields.

Mistakes - Part of the Game

The batting average of .300 in baseball is considered good, an average over .400 a nearly unachievable goal. The last player that did it was Ted Williams of the Boston Red Sox in 1941 who hit a .406. The average batter is not hitting 70% of the time! Any leader that thinks they come close to 100% perfection of their actions is kidding themselves. Mistakes are a part of taking risks, correcting them quickly is essential.

Hire the Best

Build the best team with the most talent. Leaders reward performance, go to extremes to create good working environments and use flexibility and motivation as incentives.

Communication Experts

People are awestruck by the power of good communicators. John F. Kennedy and Ronald Reagan held approval whatever party beliefs you held. Few can match that kind of dynamic presentation. But many inspire others using passion to communicate. Leaders often tell stories and use examples. Many use humility to make fun of themselves. A good sense of humor breaks the ice and brings ease and comfort to difficult situations.

A Positive Attitude

A passionate and positive attitude is critical. The focus is on individuals, be quick to compliment others.

Strategic Thinking and Problem Solving

The general who wins the battle make many calculations in his temple before the battle is fought. The general who loses makes but few calculations before hand.

—Sun Tzu

Leaders are intuitively street smart and savvy, plan well, think strategically and as a rule don't make emotional decisions. They calculate and run scenarios of what can happen, both good and bad. Leaders see problems and obstacles as part of doing business. They face up to real life situations, try to anticipate problems ahead of time and focus on the big picture.

Integrity Is Everything

Leaders respect and value of people is above all other assets. Developing trust and keeping integrity is everything.

That Peter Principle

Many think they are "entitled" to be managers. However, a promotion to a managing position for showing up or good performance does not make it right.

Eighty percent of success is showing up.
—Woody Allen

The Peter Principle is the theory that employees advance to their highest level of competence over time. Then, because they have served well or show promise, get promoted to a higher level where they are incompetent and unable to perform the new job.

The ability to hit balls over the fence and run around bases means you're a good ball player. But it *doesn't mean* you'll make a good coach. Good workers and performers aren't necessarily equipped or have the mindset to be good managers. Companies mistakenly put people in a role based on current job performance when the criteria should be, can they direct and support others? A successful transition to management is not a given and may lead to unexpected results. More people quit their jobs because of poor management than any other reason.

The Challenge

Becoming a good manager is a mindset as much as a skill. Years ago, the advantage of the hierarchal authoritative system meant managers could be successful with a big stick and a tough disposition. That made it easy to hide behind incompetence. Today, that style will bring lawsuits and trouble as we have enlightened employees and the rules have changed. This demands different tactics from managers. Workers have figured out the goal of weak managers is to keep people from noticing that they're being managed.

Most of what we call management consists of making it difficult for people to get their work done.
—Peter F. Drucker

We don't work for companies; we work for people. The manager *is* the company. The higher the skill level and talent of the worker, the more they loathe management or supervision. Capable people may be more difficult to manage, more independent and freethinking. To lead strong people it takes good leadership skills or risk losing good employees.

How to Manage Talent and Hotshots

Holding on to talent is easier said than done. It works best if you see the others point of view. The talented performers feel they volunteer their services for compensation and they won't see a manager as superior regardless of title. Managers can forget the smooth talking charisma and leave the ego at home to survive working with talented people. What works is support, not control. Superstars are productive and add value to companies. Many are creative and innovative. You can't put a price tag on these skills.

Experienced managers confident in themselves look for strength in employees, not wimp followers easy to control. Strong people losing interest in the job will look for better opportunities and stimulation. That is the main concern.

Ask questions, be an especially good listener and don't try to position hotshots as problem people or it will be even harder to manage them. The strong players are going to demand a different set of rules, however these are happy problems compared to managing incompetence.

Don't Compete with Workers

The managers' job may require constant day-to-day involvement and supervision. That's no excuse for not using good strategy and tactics. People work at peak potential when they are feeling good about what they do. Because a manager has responsibilities it does *not mean others have to share that burden.* The suspense and drama of meeting goals and quotas is the problem for the manager, not the workers. Managers are compensated for the responsibly of managing. Their job is to find innovative and creative ways to get more performance from workers. The key is to support and create good environments, not control or micro-manage.

Be Careful of Power Players

I have worked with supportive leaders and controlling managers. One way is exhilarating and the other is exasperating and debilitating. Leaders and managers looking only for power and personal gain are not the people that will help you. You do not want to work for them any longer than necessary.

> My grandfather once told me that there were two kinds of people: those who do the work and those who take the credit. He told me to try to be in the first group. There is much less competition!
>
> **—Indira Gandhi** (1917-1984)

Find leaders that have good instincts and people skills. If you are a manager, *don't compete with workers.* Every manager can employ leadership skills to enhance their performance and every worker can improve their career by learning why leaders are successful.

Improve your people skills and follow the traits of successful people. Make it a habit to read all you can about improving yourself. Take your lessons from people that have experienced success, not those who just talk or write about it. Work with strong successful people and improve your game by playing over your head. Inspired leaders help others with passion and enthusiasm.

Managers putting themselves in a position of support will themselves, gain the most.

Strong leaders that have affinity and strength, also have humility…

Remember you are just an extra in everyone else's play.
—Franklin D. Roosevelt

Steps to Success

- **Integrity Is Everything**
- **Watch What Is Done, Not What Is Said**
- **Leading And Managing Are Different Skills**
- **People Follow Leaders Because Have Confidence And Trust In Them**

Chapter 8

Plan On It-
Do What You Want

There are risks and costs to a program of action. But they are far less than the long-range risks and costs of comfortable inaction.

—**John F. Kennedy**
35th President of the United States

Often we hear people fail because they don't put goals in writing. Nonsense. People fail because they fear the uncertainty of making a decision or they simply don't know what they want to do.

Many don't know what they want until they do it, and that may be by design or luck. If you're willing to let things happen to you, you're not in control. Even worse, your luck may run out.

Become proactive. The more certain you are of what you want, the easier it becomes to take action. One of the rules the successful live by is to stick with doing what they love. That keeps them enthusiastic and passionate about success and the future. And doing what you love, keeps you moving forward.

When you gain knowledge about what you want to do, it keeps the fear of failure in perspective. The more you know, the more you will understand if your ideas and visions will really work. Some ideas are meant to be, others need to go back to the drawing board.

Before you can start a plan, you must be able to answer questions in your mind. What is it you want to accomplish and what will get you motivated to do something about it? It may sound easy but creating a vision is no small task. It takes time to acquire knowledge and think things through.

Ray Kroc was a milkshake machine salesman, with a vision, traveling the country. He was 52 years old before he started the McDonalds franchise. Bobby Fischer was 6 years old when he found instructions in a chess set bought in a candy store. Nine years later he was a chess grandmaster. My neighbor Robert Kiyosaki traveled back and forth from Phoenix to the tiny town of Bisbee, Arizona next to the Mexican border. It took him 2 years to create the *CASHFLOW* Game and write *Rich Dad, Poor Dad*. Inventors are most likely to get winning ideas in their 40's, *after years of trying.*

Visions and ideas do not have predictable limits on how old you are or how long it takes. Most people start working on visions when they realize the future is about the moves they make today. The only consistent factor is, the sooner you start, the better.

Is your goal to create passive income so you can have more free time? Do you want a career position that will let you feel you've accomplished something instead of just doing a job? Do you want to be self employed or own a business? Unless you have a business or career handed to you that you are passionate about, you must design one.

I can teach anybody how to get what they want out of life. The problem is that I can't find anybody who can tell me what they want.

—Mark Twain

Whatever vision you create, it must be real in your mind. It has to be something you really want and not just another passive thought. If you can answer yes to both of these questions, working on a plan is the next step.

Do What You Want, Don't Settle

Be sure you are creating a vision for yourself and for your own personal reasons. It's unlikely you're going to follow through on someone else's ideas or dreams. If you haven't found an idea that gets you really excited, keep looking. Don't settle for just anything that comes along. It's important to believe in this concept: creating a vision is not a game. Many great ideas are conceived from simple thoughts and visions.

Past achievements do not mean lightning will strike you twice or be a predictor of the future. No one counts your past failures but you, so leave them in the past. What your parents did or did not accomplish has little relevance to what you can accomplish. A good education and coming from a successful family can help, but it's certainly no guarantee.

How you think is your power and ultimate resource. The best thinking is what makes you passionate enough to put dreams in motion. You need only one good idea in a lifetime. No matter how many times you've tried before, the only one that counts is the one that works.

Wake Up, It's 3:00 in the Morning!

People may literally dream up their best ideas at three o'clock in the morning, and that is a fact. Sometimes your dreams are not a joke or just passing thoughts. They may give you clarity.

Your subconscious mind could be leading the way to your future. But you may have been too afraid to let yourself think you can accomplish these dreams. Your subconscious is a two-way street. It's your best supporter or your worst enemy. Your mind either sets you up or holds you back from success.

When your mind says charge and get moving, don't be so quick to rationalize with yourself. Don't lose those thoughts and ideas, they may be priceless! Keep a pad and pen next to your bed. If you wake up in the middle of the night with a great idea, write down your thoughts in detail. You never know when brilliance will strike.

While dreaming and creating a vision may have big consequences, your subconscious mind could be challenging you. Making things happen means you're going to be responsible for the results. Your conscious mind could be saying, "Yes, I can see myself doing that" while the sub-conscious mind could be saying, "Nope, there is no way I'm going to do that."

To give yourself the edge to succeed, you need a good thinking environment. A place to be calm and free of stress where you can think facts and logic.

Emotions have a way of getting facts tossed out the window. If emotions are deeply rooted you can bet they will win the argument. What we *believe* to be true and what we *know* to be true are two different things. If your emotions are in control, you may confuse fact and fiction.

A great many people think they are thinking when they are merely rearranging their prejudices.
—**William James 1842-1910**

Ideas can be big and outrageous but they still have to work. "Good ideas are the key to success," is only a half-truth. It's having a good idea that can work and *doing something about it* that creates success. It's what you do about idea's that count.

Calm in the Eye of the Storm

While living in Florida, I experienced many hurricanes. The storms have huge amounts of unpredictable energy and force. In the middle of the storms are the extreme high winds. But in the center, the eye of the storm, it's calm and quiet. In the eye of the hurricane, the sun shines in the daytime and the stars are out at night. The center is calm but surrounded by great strength. Think of where your strength is when planning.

When making important decisions, be like the calm in the center of the storm. Making big moves requires force to overcome obstacles but planning must be calm and calculated. The best time to create ideas is when you are in desire to be successful, not in need or panic that forces you to make moves you may regret later on.

You can wait for things to happen to you or you can take steps to make things happen. If you let life set your course, the odds are, you will end up average. Your odds of success improve from not so good to very good if you take your life into your own hands. People that let life run the course for them usually become the victims, not the winners.

At a college graduation ceremony Alan Greenspan at 79 years old said, "You're going to have competition, after all, before long, after my term at the Federal Reserve comes to an end, I too will be looking for a job." Hustle while you're young, it's never too early to start thinking new opportunities.

Sharp Elbows, Thick Skin and Crabs

When you put crabs in a bucket, interesting things happen. The crabs want to escape and get back to the sea. As they start trying to climb out, the others grab on to them and drag them down. People will try to pull the dreamers down as well. In the real world people have sharp elbows and will not allow others to climb out of the pot.

Conquering others requires force. Conquering oneself
requires strength.

—Lao Tzu 600 B.C.
Chinese Taoist

It takes a strong constitution to overcome the negative
attitude of others. When telling others your visions, you might
have to put up with crab-like thinking and doubt. Share your
ideas with people you trust and will support you. You need
honest feedback for ideas, not a jealous competitive reaction.

When I was young, I got regular shots of confidence. My
mother told me over and over I was going to run a big steel
company and be successful. I had no desire to get in the steel
business at 8 years old but I do remember, "You're going to be
a winner."

I also remember a manager and close friend telling me that
my newly won contract was going to pay me far above the
industry average. He said I would regret it and eventually the
company would replace me with someone for less money. I
was thinking I was adding value and performance to the
company and he was being a crab.

As you progress in business or a career, people around you
may have conflicting emotions about your success. Develop a
strong personal conviction; you will need it when you try to get
ahead of the pack.

Successful stock traders have a good lesson for all of us.
They understand a catastrophic mistake can put them out of
business. They avoid making huge mistakes by having the right
attitude and mentality. Managing emotions and accepting
failure is the most critical part of stock trading because it's
simply impossible to win all the time. Good stock traders win
only half of the time. They must be equally skilled at handling
both failure and success. Being prepared to handle things when
they go wrong is what makes great traders. The secret is cutting
losses quickly before you get in real trouble.

The key of the successful trader applies to all. When you make mistakes, keep emotions to a minimum, think clearly, and move on. You can't let life's bad experience paralyze your future: failing is part of winning.

If you've never visualized yourself successful, it might be because of a bad experience or a failure in your past. And it might be deep in your sub-conscious. You can't plan or have a vision of success if your mind is crowded with past failures.

> Whether you think that you can, or that you can't, you are usually right.
>
> **—Henry Ford**

I watched an amazing tennis match between Maria Sharapovia and Serena Williams. Maria won the Grand Slam title when she was 17 years old against an extraordinary two-time defending champion. After every shot Maria lost, it appeared as though it never happened. Williams hit booming serves but Maria shot them back and with powerful groundstrokes time after time. Maria kept a champion on her heels the whole match.

How does a 17 year old gain such remarkable maturity and talent? In a word, practice. The practice is what brings you the confidence. Your success will be plenty of matches against champions when you climb the ladder to success. More people would move forward if they weren't stuck in the past. Developing a short-term memory will help you think ahead.

Think NEXT!

When successful people lose, they become just like everyone else. Many people like to see winners crash. This is negative thinking and can stop visions of your success. *Not everything or everyone has to crash.* Setbacks are part of winning. When things go wrong, you move on and get out of things not working. An important word to add to your success vocabulary is, *NEXT!*

The assumption in many books and seminars is that people are ready to charge ahead and be successful. That is not true. You need to be in the right mindset to make positive moves. People are held back from success and moving ahead because they are in *the wrong mindset.* Change the paradigm that being successful is selling out. It's not. Everyone is entitled to go for a better life and dream bigger dreams regardless of the past.

Creating a dream and a vision is the first step to success and the future. After developing a vision, you work on a plan to make your ideas reality. Life gets exciting once you make that commitment.

People talk a good game but few make the moves to get things accomplish. When you stop talking and make a commitment to take action, something interesting usually happens. Family and friends will rally in your support and help you.

> Your time is limited; so don't waste it living someone else's life. Don't be trapped by dogma - which is living with the results of other people's thinking. Don't let the noise of other's opinions drown out your own inner voice. And most important, have the courage to follow your heart and intuition. They somehow already know what you truly want to become. Everything else is secondary.
>
> **—Steve Jobs**
> CEO, Apple

A modern day warrior was using 2,500-year old Chinese strategies and few had a clue. Read ahead as Woody shows how business is a game of strategic thinking and planning.

Steps to Success

- **Let The Past Be That**
- **Don't Let Others Distract You**
- **Do What You Want And Don't Settle**
- **Get Over Old Paradigms And Move On**
- **Plans Start With A Vision Or A Dream**

Chapter 9

Think Strategically-
Outwit & Outsmart

The future belongs to those who see possibilities before they
become obvious.

—John Sculley
Former CEO Pepsi and Apple Computer

You go from nowhere to somewhere with one good idea.
Rewards for taking action on what you believe in can be
extraordinary. Strategy turns thoughts into reality.

Story of a Plan

In the late 1960s and early 1970s, AM radio and 8-track
players ruled. Broadcasters considered FM a poor stepchild to
AM and gave it little attention. However, some were seeing
opportunities on the FM dial. Underground album rock on FM
was getting the attention of young listeners. And a new idea for
adult listeners was in play. They called it "Easy Listening" and
well suited for FM stereo.

Jim Schulke was on the creative edge developing this
concept and had experience in radio sales as well. His
understanding how radio ratings were calculated and computed
gave him programming insight. He was one of the first to

figure out how to program a radio format that would not only appeal to listeners, but also maximize rating potential.

Jim created a small company called SRP, Schulke Radio Productions and hired creative programmers to help him produce the format. It wasn't just about good programming, it was a bigger play. It was FM stations overtaking AM stations using programming and marketing tactics taking advantage of technology. FM produced a quality FM sound superior to AM and it was about to get exploited.

Think Tall

In 1969 Woody Sudbrink bought WWPB FM in Miami. The call letters changed to WLYF FM and the antenna was moved to the top of a TV tower on the Dade Broward County line. The new signal at 1,000 feet reached north of Palm Beach to the Florida Keys. Woody bought stations in the early transition period of the late 1960s and early 1970s.

FM stations in major markets were sold for what they call stick value, or a fraction of their real worth. Woody was putting a broadcasting group together buying FM stations in Miami, Baltimore, Cincinnati, Milwaukee, Chicago, Philadelphia and Atlanta. All of the stations had excellent signals or the potential to have good coverage. Not many people paid attention to what Woody was doing and few understood his strategy. Who would want FM stations when AM stations had virtually all the listeners? Woody was also acquiring small AM religious stations.

The corporate offices were in Ft. Lauderdale with five full time people. Hal Gore was the President and senior broadcaster. Woody and Hal managed the company with a sharp focus. Keep expenses low, produce a quality sound and aggressively market the stations. They hired General Managers to put all the effort into sales. Woody himself focused on marketing and engineering and worked on being sure the best and latest technology was at every station.

Deals Are Made When You Buy

The plan was simple. Buy stations cheaply, improve them, and sell them for a much higher price. Woody told me the best deals are made when you buy something because you never assume you can sell anything for more than market value. If you want to change that rule, you have to add value to what you bought. Therefore, you work hard to buy at the right price. Woody would say, "Run our stations like we will own them forever. We might have to."

Part of the strategic plan was all the stations use a single source of programming. That would ensure cost control and maintain quality programming. Woody contracted with Jim of SRP programming for the easy listening music service to run on all the FM stations in the group.

One of the tactics was to strictly limit the number of commercials per hour and be sure the advertisers message fit the easy music sound. Loud intrusive commercials were rejected, many advertisers had to re-do commercials or they were not allowed on the station. Everything that went on the air had to fit the sound of the format.

FM sound quality was superior to AM radio and the soft quality music filled a need. As the format was not intrusive, it was being played where noisy commercial formats were not welcome. Professional offices, retail stores, restaurants and people in cars found the new radio format and began playing the soft easy music all day long. A steady stream of listeners called the station every day and thanked the station for the service.

As the rating service had a natural bias for long listening, the addition of in-office radio listeners along with in car listening could tip the scales and make the new FM format the highest rated in the market. A loyal audience that stays with a station longer has the potential to make ratings soar.

Aggressive marketing of the new radio stations on TV, billboards, buses and bus benches quickly created listener awareness. Advertising the radio station had an additional advantage. People would find it easier to remember the call letters and dial location of the station. The concept was "aided recall." People that saw the radio station advertising had little confusion remembering what radio station they were listening to should a rating service include them in a survey. The slogans and "positioning" of the stations were designed to be deceptively simple and easy to remember. In Miami, "WLYF Is Beautiful, FM 101.5, All Music, All the Time," ran every commercial interruption.

Few competitors had any concept of what was going on and did not understand the strategy. This was out of the box thinking and ahead of it's time. Competitors were blind to what was happening. They called the new radio formats uncreative, boring and a sea of music that was just like a tape machine with limited commercials. They nicknamed the stations, "Music of Your Death." They said it was not real radio.

Only the Listeners Liked the Station

The audience however, had a different viewpoint. The format had little DJ chatter. For many however, the quiet commercial breaks with less talk were perfect. People outside the radio business saw the advantage but inside the business, it was ignored and disliked. The changes were too new and radical.

Innovations often perform worse than leading technology or products when they start and insiders often miss the signs. The way to be sure this is not happening to your company or product, follow two rules:

If you want an opinion about your company or your competition, you need to ask people outside of your business and company.

If you want to know if things are changing, you need to ask people that have no stake in your company.

These rules are so simple and logical it is hard to imagine a business could overlook this fact. However, many businesses do overlook them and get stuck in paradigms of their past success. Many successful businesses will not allow themselves to see different ways of doing things or pay attention to competitors. When people cannot see the forest through the trees, they will not see lumberjacks coming either.

Woody was programming for new listeners to a new kind of radio. He figured out how he was going to get the rating credit he was entitled. It was brilliant yet simple. Good business plans are easy to understand and you know you can follow through on them because you can see how they are going to work. Complicated things made simple are the key when planning. Genius is making the difficult easy to understand. The overview of a good business plan should fit on a 3 x 5 index card.

These Guys are Different

I moved from New York to Miami. I had a wife, a son and a new baby on the way. Radio sales seemed to be the best career move and I took a job at a small AM station to get started. I noticed a new FM radio station in the market with a big advertising campaign. It appeared to be advertising more than all the other radio stations in the market combined. I could see this station was going to be something special and I liked the format. However, it had virtually no listeners or ratings.

Steve, the manager of this new station heard I was new in town and called me to meet for a game of tennis.

"You should meet the owners of this new company. The guys that own the company are a little unusual but I think you'll like them," Steve said. He set up a meeting in November of 1971 and I met with Woody and Hal. The meeting went well and I was comfortable with the style. These guys *are* real entrepreneurs, I thought.

"Well, do you have radio in your blood?" Woody said.

"No, I have new babies and mortgages in my blood. I want to be successful and pay the bills. I can sell your station and format, no problem." I said.

"Let's do this!" Hal jumped in.

I joined the company on the spot. I started at WLYF FM as a salesperson with a promise of advancement if things worked out. As the station had few accounts on the air, I could call on any of the advertising agencies in Miami.

"I just took a job at the new station. We're taking a risk here, but if it works, it will be a home run," I told my wife.

One month later, I was out with Steve making sales calls. We stopped for lunch at a bar and grill on Biscayne Boulevard in downtown Miami. They had a free phone for regular customers; we could have a quick sandwich, get our messages from the office and be on our way.

Steve called the office and got a message. The fall radio ratings were out. Call the sales representative immediately. Steve called New York. He had a bar napkin to write on, his hand started to shake, he could hardly write.

He was saying "11, we have an 11."

I said, "11 what?"

He said, "That's our share!" Steve was saying on the phone, "Are you sure? The station is number one?"

We raced back to the station to get all the ratings and figure out what happened. We were asking ourselves, was this possible? The first FM station in history to become number one over all AM and FM stations in a big market? Word was on the street like wildfire. The competition was calling the advertising agencies and saying the ratings were bogus and a fluke. It was impossible and there was simply no way to explain it, they said.

My New Boss

It was a few months later and I found myself with a new boss. He was a little older and like myself had come from the advertising business in New York. We had so many similar qualities we clashed. Norm however was great fun and as we were so focused on success, it all started to work. The funny thing was we looked like each other.

I called Norman and said, "I'm writing a book and need those stories you've been telling everyone for years."

"Deal!" Norman said and wrote, "Brian & I took our first trip to New York together to visit our rep firm. We entered the building and took the elevator to go up to the rep firm. For some unknown reason, I stood in one back corner of the elevator and Brian stood in the other back corner. As we were waiting for the elevator doors to close, in shuffled a deliveryman carrying one of those large portfolio folders. As he entered the elevator, he stopped, glanced over to me and then glanced over to Brian and exclaimed 'Brothers,' turned around and rode the elevator with us as Brian and I roared."

After we made sales calls together, the market started to call us "Frick and Frack." And Norman's favorite cement truck story:

As he normally did, Woody Sudbrink, owner of our station was reviewing the monthly bills and noticed that there was a charge for an automobile on the list.

"What's that for?" Woody said.

"That's for Brian's car." I said.

"We shouldn't be paying for that," Woody said.

"Hey, that was what the deal was when we hired him, so we have to honor that," I said.

"What kind of a car," he then asked.

"Buick Riviera," I said.

"That's too expensive, get him a Pinto." Woody said.

So we got Brian a Pinto, which of course, was so underpowered, its air conditioning could not handle the 95 degree Miami temperature. Brian was a very unhappy camper. One day, coming back from calls, I noticed this anguished look on Brian's face, he was red as a beet and sweat was pouring down his face. I just knew that the second I asked, "What's wrong, Brian," I was going to get it, but being adventurous,

"What's wrong?" I said to Brian...and he exploded like Mt. Vesuvius.

"I'm not giving my life up for this company," he went on for 5 minutes. I did all I could to keep from busting out laughing since I knew the minute I asked, "What's wrong?" he would tell me.

Coming back from a sales call in his little Pinto (in 95 degree temperature) he came upon a traffic jam and almost didn't stop in time. As he looked in his rear view mirror, he saw a cement truck bearing down on him. Its engine compartment was very high and looked like a nose on someone's face. The truck stopped barely in time with Brian's whole Pinto directly under the engine of the cement truck. If the truck had a normal front end, it would have crushed Brian's Pinto. We got Brian a new car.

Norman and I wrote FM history as the station succeeded beyond everyone's wildest expectations. The risk I took with a new company and an unknown product paid off. It was an important lesson for me and I was about to get a lot more. As time went on and things unfolded, I began to see the strategy.

Don't Chew Up the People

In October 1974, I met with Woody and Hal. We were at a McDonalds in Ft. Lauderdale where we had most of our corporate meetings. Woody had on a casual Ban Lon shirt and a tan from walking on the beach; Hal was a great dresser, wore expensive shoes, but no socks. The "Boys," as we called them, were a new entrepreneurial corporate style.

I was being promoted to manager of WLIF FM in Baltimore. It was going to be confusing going from WLYF FM Miami to WLIF FM Baltimore. Aside from the different call letters, the formats and music were the same. I was young, inexperienced as a manager and did not want to leave Miami. However, this was a great opportunity.

Our corporate meeting started.

"Now Brian, here's what you do. Run the business out of your back pocket. And don't chew up the people," Woody said. The meeting was over in no time and we had lunch with lots of small talk.

You had to understand how to read between the lines. The company was saying sell the most advertising you can, do not spend a dime you don't have to, keep the people happy and don't mess with things you don't understand.

This was a very hands-off style of leadership, the company had you focused on the strategic plan, "Make the numbers!" No one had the time or desire to over-manage people. The plan was to drive the car as fast as you can, just didn't drive it off the road.

When I got to Baltimore, I found the station in Towson, an upscale community north of the city. The offices were in a small converted ranch house. A long winding road led to the clearing, the station was on 14 acres surrounded by trees. Broadcast studios were in the bedrooms, transmitters in the cellar and sales desks in the hallway.

The station was programmed Beautiful Music with very limited commercials, the same as in all the Sudbrink markets. A 1,000-foot broadcasting tower was on top of a hill in the center of the property. This was one of the best FM signals in all of Maryland.

After I was in the new job, I realized I had not gotten a phone call or memo in over two months from the corporate office. I sent sales reports every Friday and that was all the updates they needed. This style of managing with my inexperience was unnerving but I realized they were teaching me how to swim by throwing me overboard without a life ring. I learned how to run a business in a hurry.

On our property was a short AM tower that also belonged to our company. The AM studios were in a small one room storefront office in a shopping center. The programming was religion and they sold block time and advertising to churches and ministers. The broadcasting and recording equipment was on card tables and looked like it came from a 1940's science fiction movie, everything was older than I was.

I met the manager of the religious station and the full time staff of three. In spite of the size of this tiny radio station, it was very busy making money. In the radio business, you call profits Cash Flow. This tiny station was making a lot of Cash Flow and it was off the competitive radar screen.

After meeting the manager it occurred to me that we had other religious AM stations in our company all doing the same thing. I had not given it much thought until that meeting. In our company we didn't talk about the AM stations, it seemed we had little in common. Or did we?

Time went on, WLIF in Baltimore become a huge success and at one point, the highest rated FM Major Market station in the U.S. We had a tiny staff of 11 full time people and we made extremely good Cash Flow for the company. That kept everyone very happy, until the end. Woody sold the station in Baltimore; he was selling all the stations.

By 1977 Woody had sold the entire radio group. The format that made the Sudbrink Company so successful was showing cracks and problems. The timing to sell the group of stations was good, it was time to take profits and move on. But Woody was already working on a new plan to buy different kinds of stations in different formats.

Success May Blind You

Many smart business people missed a phenomenal opportunity getting into FM radio when it had little perceived value. But, at the time, it appeared things in the radio business were going along fine and only AM stations had real value. It is when you think things are most secure that the unlikely is most likely to happen. If you're on the edge and looking to stay sharp in a career or business, you watch to see new things coming and check to see if old things are changing.

It's when you get comfortable that you can get into trouble in business and careers. Woody, as a creative businessman, saw the FM radio business from a new perspective. He maximized the rating potential going after a new audience with innovative marketing and leading edge technology. His vision was perfectly clear; he was not thinking like everyone else. He was on the edge of new thinking.

Woody had confidence his plan was good, but it was still a risk. No matter how many times you calculate a plan, the risk is undetermined and only calculated. Without prior experience of doing the exact same plan, you can only make an intelligent guess as to how long a new business or turnaround takes to work and become successful.

The secret in planning is not only what you know; *it's how to handle what you don't know.*

Woody had the religious stations making money to help cover the FM stations losses. Business losses were calculated but not how long the losses would continue. As long as the business had a backup plan to cover expenses, it could go on for years. The risk of the plan taking time to work had been factored in. You need a good blueprint to build a house; you need a good plan to run a business.

The vision, plan, strategy and tactics were textbook. *Inside Radio* reported "Sudbrink originally purchased then unpopular FM stations for very little money and made a whopping $24 million profit in 1977." In 1977, that was a big number for a tiny company to make.

The View from the Top

Only a few at the top of a business see the entire business strategy as it's planned. People *in* the business get to see parts of the plan but many don't get to experience putting it all together.

Lack of experience creating plans stops people from trying new strategies and ventures. The unknown creates the fear of failure and the risk stops most people from even trying. But it's more lack of knowledge than ability that stops people. The more you know about what you want to do, the better your vision, the easier it is to start a plan. You must have determination and a willingness to learn new things. Taking steps in a new direction is only as scary as the *lack of knowledge*.

> Risk comes from not knowing what you're doing.
> **—Warren Buffett**

A good plan is the first step to success and no one has a lock on new ideas and visions. Woody bought radio stations for the price of a tract home in Los Angeles because he saw the value. That's what you call vision.

Planning for Risk Makes it Safer

The more experienced you become, the more you appreciate that risk is always a part of the equation. We get no free lunch. Preparing for risk lets you move forward and the worst thing that can happen may not be so bad. The more you conceive of what can go wrong, the more you can control the risk. If you plan for unexpected things to happen, you are in control. You start with a good plan by putting all the options on the table and pretend you're in strange waters. When you start out, be sure your feet touch the ground and your head is above water.

Many people are not going to be motivated to quit a job and start a venture. Many people should not think that way if they enjoy what they are doing and are able to achieve the lifestyle they enjoy. Being an entrepreneur is not for everyone.

However in business today, you need to *think like an entrepreneur* as the business world is setting new rules. Companies expect you to bring more to the table and help solve problems, not bring more problems.

Use the same rules for improving a career as planning a business. Careers don't suddenly get better by accident; you plan your steps to achieve goals just like a business plans its future. Successful people live the dream and plan for good things to happen by their actions, not by accident.

Strategies for Planning

When I started making annual plans and budgets, I was filling in blank spaces and following instructions. The companies were actually doing the planning; I was confirming what had been estimated. However, it was still my plan to follow. The education for me was putting in the numbers and details.

There is no better way to learn about planning than to roll up your sleeves and do it. This was excellent training and I learned what worked, and what didn't, as the plan went into action. As I took on more responsibilities, I learned more. I was able to create entire plans and concepts; my skills improved with time and practice.

Friendly Competition Became War

Commercial research came to the radio industry in the late 1970s. Determining what people listened to and learning about music preference had been the majority of research for most broadcasters. As the industry matured new tools and strategies came into play. The tactics turned to marketing warfare and radio formats competitively positioned for maximum success. Researching the competition and the marketplace became essential.

A cottage industry of researchers formed to serve the radio industry. Researchers introduced broadcasters to the strategic thinking and strategies of Sun Tzu, the Chinese warrior-philosopher, and Carl von Clausewitz, the Prussian soldier intellectual.

War strategy brought dramatic results. Clear-cut winners and losers emerged immediately. Radio stations using perceptual research and tactical strategies were beating the pants off the unprepared. A sleepy business became cutting edge.

Twenty-five hundred years ago, Sun Tzu wrote the "Art of War" and the work is still a contemporary tool. Businesses and political leaders read the interpretations; the Chinese strategies translated into virtually every language. Legend is Napoleon studied the work and claimed it the key to victories in Europe. Rommel studied it in North Africa and Lee Iacocca read it. The strategies are based on the concept that warfare is deception and this can be a brilliant strategy in business.

> Thus, when able to attack, we must seem unable. Hold out bait to entice the enemy. Feign disorder, and crush him. If he is in superior strength, evade him. If your opponent is quick to anger, seek to irritate him. Pretend to be weak, that he may grow arrogant.
>
> **—Sun Tzu**

Don't Fight: Outwit & Outsmart

Warfare is not just about battle, its inner strength and personal wisdom. A quarterback in a football game plays a game of deception but does not think his actions are deceptive or immoral; *it's how the game is played.* Wisdom comes from knowing that in the dead of winter and freezing temperatures, it's not a good idea to send troops into battle. Many will get frostbite and warriors will lose their fingers. It is best to wait for warmer weather or look for other options.

Sun Tzu strategy points out direct confrontation may bring destruction. *Do not get on a battlefield if you do not have to.* As a warrior and strategist, you win victory and create success with personal skills and smart strategic thinking.

The mind is power. You calculate, think, plan, outwit and outmaneuver opponents and obstacles. You do everything you can to win without battle; *you are planning to win before you start.* If you are not confident your ideas and plans can win, consider alternatives. Strategic thinking leads to clarity in actions.

Leaders Wear Many Hats

War, as a business strategy, flies in the face of win-win sensitive thinking. But this thinking depends on the role you play in your business or your company. If you are the CEO, President or Key Executive, your strategic thinking may bring success to the entire organization. Revenues, market share and competitors are the concern; profit is the lifeline of business. A company that is not able to produce a profit and return on investment will soon be history and out of business.

The work environment and employee welfare is a critical part of strategy, happy employees are more productive. People take pride and enjoyment in what they do and most people enjoy being part of a team. For many, camaraderie on the job is as important as family life.

But workers' welfare is on a different strategic level than planning or running a business for profit and success.

> **Working in the business and on the business are two different skills.**

Leaders have to live with competitors that want to eat them for lunch *yet* must be sensitive and supportive to workers at the same time. The workplace is competitive, success is not a given.

> **Creating a good work environment is both an offensive and defensive strategy.**

Only the Beginning

Writing a plan is the not the end of the planning process, it's only the beginning. Getting to your goals and realizing what you want to do is why you plan. The purpose of writing a plan is to get ideas on paper. You must be able to follow what you want to accomplish. A plan has to be detailed enough to get the job done. If you alone are using the plan, suit your personal needs. If others are to use the plan, you have to make it easy to understand. Overdoing a plan is time consuming and not productive. A plan is a roadmap, not a legal document. It needs to be flexible as events dictate.

When you write ideas on paper, your subconscious mind has a positive reminder every time the plan is reviewed. However, it's far more important to write ideas and strategies on a napkin and stick it on the refrigerator than it is to think about writing an elaborate plan that never gets done.

Understanding the thinking of a business plan helps you position your skills within the business. At the very least, you can understand how effective your company is in getting to its goals. You may have more to contribute to your job and company if you understand how the planning process works.

Are We Seeing Right?

We all live in our own paradigms. A paradigm is a set of assumptions and concepts; it's a reality for those ideas. Paradigms are common and useful but they can blind you to creative ideas or solutions. It's called a "Paradigm Effect" and means you can be too close to things. The invention of the quartz electric watch is a classic paradigm story.

The Swiss for centuries were world-class quality watchmakers. Thousands worked in the profession creating beautiful watches with quality few other countries or manufactures could match. Around 1960, the Swiss invented an electronic watch, a quartz timepiece. It was accurate but of no use to anyone. It had no gears, precious stones and hand-made details. The Swiss thinking was who would want such a simple watch. Visiting executives from Japan were in Switzerland and shown this new invention. They saw something different than the Swiss were seeing. Different cultures and people can have different visions and mindsets. As this quartz watch had no perceived value to the Swiss, the Japanese were able to buy the rights for a small price.

It did not take long for the Japanese to figure out how to make accurate watches for very little money. They brought excellent timepieces to the marketplace for a tiny fraction of the cost of Swiss watches. Japanese manufacturers gained an edge in the watch industry and the Swiss watchmakers lost the leadership and thousands of jobs. A new market created, an old market was re-positioned. More people could now afford an accurate watch and a new disruptive technology changed the industry overnight. The Swiss were blinded by success.

What is Your Edge?

What is the unique benefit or advantage you have that will help your career? Is it your experience or education? Is it the years of insight at your job or your understanding of how your company works? Can you understand why your competition is successful or failing? Can you identify your edge? If you don't have an edge, start working on one. The smallest advantage in a competitive workplace can be the difference between a cubicle and an office with a window.

A trader in stocks uses skills and knowledge to see patterns in charts. They capitalize on that ability to forecast winners. A business can do the same by studying patterns in the business and marketplace. When you shop at Nordstroms, you have a unique experience with someone playing a piano. When you buy a Lexus you are inundated with unique service and follow up. When you eat at Ruth's Chris or Morton's restaurants, you can feel and taste the unique advantage of fine food and great service. Look for leading businesses to changes the rules; look for the best of breed to set the pace.

Many businesses run just to stay in business. For a business to go beyond average, it must have an edge or unique advantage. Many people in business work hard in the business, but do not see *outside* of the business. If you're not sure about a position in the market, hire people or do your own research to find that advantage. Find an edge or create one, it's a key part of the strategic planning.

Paradigms

Everyone has paradigms, understand them to help your strategies:

Paradigm paralysis prevents us from seeing or accepting changes.

"Paradigm Effect" blinds you to creative solutions.

Outsiders may see opportunities insiders don't look for. Old habits can prevent insiders from seeing new opportunities.

Outsiders have no vested interest in keeping things the same or following traditions.

Be prepared for outsiders to change our thinking for us if we miss opportunities.

Better and more productive ideas will come to the market if people see a new opportunity exists.

You don't want to get in a business or career because that's all you know. *You want to do something you know will work.* You may have to learn new skills in order to move forward. Sun Tzu teaches us to contain ego, emotion and politics when planning, be calm and think strategic. When implementing the plan and taking action, that is time to get excited. Calm strategic thinking and emotional energy both have a time and a place.

Make Time for Homework

Research your ideas as best you can. This can be as simple as asking a dozen people an opinion or you can poll hundreds of people through strategic research projects. You can learn from listening to people in a focus group or you can go to a mall and ask people questions. The Internet gives you information from all over the planet, virtually free. Gathering data is math and science. That is the easy part of research.

The difficult part of research is the human element, the not so precise side. If you ask the wrong questions, you get confirmations on the wrong answers. Designing research to confirm what you think may be satisfying to the ego but lead you in the wrong direction.

Questions need to get you information on what people think or what markets need. If you are not eager to find real answers, your competitors might see your mistakes and find your weakness before you do. Ask questions about your strength and ask questions to discover your weakness.

If you get good data and you interpret your findings well, you are miles ahead of anyone who does not have this information. However, if you interpret good data incorrectly, you are just as wrong as if you had bad information. Be careful not to read into your findings things that do not exist. Do not stretch data and findings to confirm theories.

Study Your Competitors

Researching competitors may be the fastest and easiest track to success. Knowing your competition can be just as important as knowing your customers. Your competitors may give you a blueprint of what to do. Or just as important, *what not to do.* The more you know about your competition, the easier the decisions will be to go after them *or stay away from them.* Try to discover weaknesses, if any, but also understand strengths. Offensive or defensive may be an opportunity. When you understand your competition, you can better decide how to improve or change your position.

The following ideas are proven strategies and tactics to help you formulate a plan. What position you are in and what control you have directs your planning. You are not alone in a business or a career, surroundings, opposition and competition is part of a plan.

What is Your Position, Where are You?

Defense-You're on top of the hill, you defend your position at all costs. You save your energy and let useless attacks against you happen (but you have to know the difference between useful and useless attacks). To defend yourself, you attack your strengths and weakness before your opposition figures them out. You do research on yourself like your competitor will do on you! You never let your guard down and never assume the offense is weak (but never assume they are stronger than they really are). Use your power against the opposition at the right time. That will bring more power. To prevent a possible attack from coming at you, your best defense is to have your enemy thinking you're crazy enough to do anything to stop them. In today's competitive environment, leaders defending positions must be at the forefront of innovation and creativity and can't rest or be satisfied with success.

Offense-You are not on top of the hill but you are going after the leader. The concern is how *strong* is the leader? Go after the most vulnerable point in the service or product. Look for a technical breakthrough. Keep offense narrow and broaden only on success. Try to catch the leader off-guard. Go all out when attacking the market leaders.

Flanking - If you're new to the market or a small player trying to get bigger, flanking is a good strategy. Move to an uncontested area. Look for bigger players to drop the ball, go after holes in the market. This can be especially effective as you might not have to spend anything on marketing. Surprise is your strongest element. Do what your opposition thinks you won't do. Attack narrow and keep it concentrated, don't get fancy and broaden your attack if you're flanking. Run like crazy, pursuit is more important than the attack itself, it will catch your opposition off-guard.

Gorilla - Companies or individuals that control a small niche. Gorillas are upstarts that combine offense, defense, and flanking on a small scale. Think of Budweiser beer with nationwide distribution competing against a one location tiny microbrewery that makes its own beer in Breckenridge, Colorado. Gorillas are very tiny players, fast and able to move at lightning speed and will do anything to stay alive.

Making Things Happen

Use research to support and help decide the best way to get a plan into action. Are you going to start a new business with no competitors or go after the competition? Are you in a business that is doing well or at the bottom looking to improve a problem? Is your career on track or off track? Look at the strategies of both offense and defense to decide what tactics to take and how to implement a plan.

Set your goals. Even if your plan is a one-pager, you still need goals and strategies tied to a timetable and real numbers. Goals have to be reasonable, time bound, and measurable.

A good accountant is critical, you need someone smart and well informed to run the numbers and be sure a plan can work. Legal help will keep your plan out of trouble. If you're planning a career move that involves a contract or agreement, get professional help. If you're getting into a business or industry that's already established, go to trade meetings and meet operators.

Write your plan and you're ready to take action. It's impossible to cover all you need to write a plan. But all plans start with a way of thinking. The important thing *is getting started* and use strategic thinking.

You are the architect of the plan; you create the blueprint of what you want to build. Plans simple and easy to follow are the ones that work the best, do not over think and complicate things. A good plan is great but a good plan easy to follow will build a better business or career.

Creating a Brand

Robert Kiyosaki, author of the *Rich Dad, Poor Dad* series, is the number one business author in America today. Yet Robert claims that he is a best selling author, not a best writing author. And that his real success is due to his years of studying how to not only write books, but how to market and sell them.

"To be in business or be an entrepreneur today, you have to realize the number one skill is selling," said Robert. An extraordinary story follows about taking action...and making a sale.

Steps to Success

- **Think Strategically**
- **You Need A Plan To Follow**
- **Does Your Plan Have An Edge?**
- **Don't Fight: Outwit & Outsmart**
- **Calculating The Risk Is Part Of Winning**
- **Plan Offense And Defense, You Can Win Either Way**
- **Understand Paradigms To See Opportunities**

Chapter 10

Take Action-
Rock 'n' Roll

You miss 100% of the shots you never take.
—Wayne Gretzky

Taking action means changes and the unknown, the natural reaction is to resist it. The very things that make us nervous and uncomfortable also make us winners. Overcoming inertia and getting things moving is no easy task.

Taking action is so important even the gifted, educated and talented lose advantage without motivation and drive. Talk is cheap, things happen when desire and passion overcome fear and failure. Being energetic, proactive and enthusiastic is the engine for success. Nothing happens from all our efforts unless we are willing do something.

The squad in the locker room quietly studies the plans and competition. Once the players hit the field, the calm is over. Never underestimate a passionate team excited about doing something. You may get run over by sheer emotion, adrenaline, and energy. The goal is to be on the winning team, not the learning team milling around trying to figure out what to do. Surround yourself with winners and they will help you move forward.

In war as in business, different strategies and tactics require different behavior. Not everything goes along in an even monotone fashion. Getting a plan into action is one of those times when you need to shift gears. Moving from calm thinking and strategy to energy and emotion is a major shift in attitude. If you think you can be successful because you are a good thinker and ride on that skill alone, you are in for a learning experience. Ten percent brains and ninety percent perspiration separate the successful from the average. To be a winner, get your heart rate up and go for it, just as if you're getting ready to run a race.

Rock 'n' Roll

Sudbrink had sold the Beautiful Music FM stations and was buying new ones to put rock 'n' roll formats on the air. In 1978, I re-joined the company and moved to Orlando, Florida to manage WORJ FM. The station was bought out of bankruptcy. We changed the format to Album Rock and called it ZETA7, it was rated dead last in the market.

I met with David Sousa our program director.

"How are we going to get this station off the ground? Without promotion, people won't find out what we're doing," I said. In Florida, license tags are only required on the back of cars, you could put whatever you wanted on the front of your car. David said, "Let's buy license plates to put them on the front of our listeners' cars. No other radio station in the market is doing it, we'll have an advantage with a head start just in case anyone tries to copy us. The idea worked in Miami at ZETA4." We called a meeting and everyone liked the idea. But the staff was afraid if we gave the license plates away, they would wind up in college dorms and kids' bedrooms, not on cars. That would not get the radio station visibility. I suggested putting tags on cars should be a station promotion. We would have the radio station staff go out to shopping malls on weekends and put the license plates on ourselves. That way, we would know the tags would wind up on cars.

Bolt On's

"I have an idea. We'll call the promotion a 'Bolt On.' We'll tell listeners to come to our promotion to get a free tag. And we'll bolt the plate on for them."

Everyone thought the "Bolt On" idea was a winner; we had our first big promotion to kick off the new radio format.

I ordered 30,000 license tags. When the plates arrived, it took hours to unload the truck. We were excited, but when I saw all those boxes, I got nervous. I was worried I ordered too many tags, but no turning back now.

Andy our chief salesman found a shopping mall in the center of Orlando willing to give us an open parking area on a Saturday morning. We put promotional announcements on the air and invited listeners for free drinks, sub sandwiches and a free ZETA7 license tag.

"You don't have to get out of the car, we'll 'Bolt On' the license plates for you," we said on the radio. Bright red cones were lined up like a long snake in the parking lot to direct cars. We had a small staff on hand to see how this would work; we had no idea what kind of turnout to expect.

As soon as the promotion started, it created a traffic jam that flowed out to the entrance of the mall. People could not find parking spaces and the mall called the police to help direct traffic.

"What a surprise," people at the mall said, "like the day before Christmas." The station was invited to do more promotions.

The next weekend we were better prepared with more staff as we knew what was going to happen. We had sunscreen, folding chairs, umbrellas. We did this promotion every

Saturday for weeks before we took a rest. By that time, ZETA7 license tags were on cars everywhere.

> The surprising and the straightforward give rise to each other as they rotate and cycle without end. Who can exhaust them?
>
> **—Sun Tzu**

Our competition was stunned; it was too late to react. ZETA7 was easily the most visible station in Orlando and people surprised how quickly this happened.

You could spot the ZETA tags everywhere. People came to the radio station during the week to pick up free tags. It was obvious many would never even listen to a rock radio station but they still wanted a license tag. What is a ZETA they would ask? We told them it was the sixth letter of the Greek alphabet and we were just borrowing it for a while. We had an 80-year-old grandma with a pink Cadillac come to the station asking for her tag as long as we put it on the car for her.

A tag on the back of a car is only a fraction as visible as a tag on the front of a car. If you sit in traffic or drive a highway, you see only the license plate of the immediate car in front of you. But the oncoming traffic is visible from a long distance, and you can see *all* the cars coming at you. Car after car had the black, yellow and red ZETA7 jumping out at you. People with tags were waving at each other as if they were in the same fraternity.

A local TV station gave ZETA7 priceless publicity when they discovered, "Public vehicles had radio station license tags on them." The TV station had cameras on an overpass in the center of Orlando during afternoon drive. It seemed like every third or fourth car had a ZETA7 tag. The news cast continued, "Police cars, fire engines and ambulances are not supposed to be advertising a radio station. This is city property," they said.

This made the radio station even more popular, the ratings jumped on the marketing. The enthusiasm of the disk jockeys made the programming even better. ZETA7 became the number one Album Rock radio station in Orlando and central Florida. Advertising sales soared.

Sliding Into the Pacific Ocean

It was spring of 1980, Woody asked me to transfer to Honolulu. I was to manage KDUK FM. The format was out of tune with the market, sales were slow, and nothing they tried seemed to work. Local management had changed the famous KPOI call letters to KDUK, the station had lost all identity. I changed the format to Album Rock and called the station "98Rock." We changed the call letters back to KPOI.

We were creating TV commercials to promote the new station when the production company called and said, "Where is the 98Rock logo? We need it now!" We had no time to meet deadlines. I took a wide marker and scribbled the 98Rock to make it look like it had been painted from a fat paintbrush. I found a local artist to clean up my artwork and it turned out to be a hit. We won a Pele Award from the Honolulu Advertising Federation for best logo design in the state.

Well, I thought, at least we got that part right. Now if we can only get the radio station to sound as good as the logo, we'll be moving. I convinced "Mr. Bill" Mims to move to Hawaii to program the station and get the music on track.

I was all set to do a similar license tag promotion as we had done at ZETA7, but in Hawaii, license tags are on both the front and back of the cars. We had to find another way to promote the station and our new rock format.

We were so far behind the other stations we hit our lowest point when concert promoters from Los Angeles told us, "Don't bother." They would not even let us do free promotions for rock events. They said the station was, "That bad."

What's a Surfer Wallet?

One day in the mail I received a promotional wallet from a rock station in Atlanta, Georgia. The wallet was made of nylon with Velcro zippers. It was black with a bright white and yellow logo. What a great idea I thought, this is perfect for our audience. I called the rock radio station in Atlanta to find out who was making the wallets for them.

"The company is in your back yard, we're ordering the wallets from a company called Rippers in Honolulu," they told me. I hung up the phone, called information and found Rippers a few miles from our office. I called them.

"I'm coming right over, I have an idea for us," I said.

I walked into Rippers. One lady was making a hat. All the long rows of sewing machines stood empty. The factory was very quiet. At the end of this room was a desk and two men were talking. I went to meet them.

"I'm Robert Kiyosaki. You must be Brian from the radio station. What can we do for you?"

"I want to put our 98Rock logo on your surfer wallets and give them away as a promotion," I said as I explained my idea. I ordered 100 wallets, gave them logo artwork and asked how long it would take to make them. Robert said, "It won't take long, as you can see we're not very busy."

When the wallets were delivered, we give them away on the air. Immediately, we got a reaction. The phone lines to the station lit up non-stop. Listeners were calling to buy the wallets. They were not asking for them free. I heard about KMEL FM in San Francisco selling merchandise and had an old friend at the station. I called Mike Brandt the General Sales Manager to get details.

"We're selling mostly T-shirts, but we have other things like logo key chains, baseball hats and tank tops. Retail stores order merchandise from the station and we support them with promotions," Mike said. It's a good program for everyone and listeners had no problem paying for the "KMEL GEAR" merchandise.

Nope, It Won't Work

I asked our staff what they thought about selling station T-shirts to listeners.

"Not a good idea," was the answer. Everyone warned me, "This will not work! Promotional T-shirts are supposed to be free." But that's old thinking, I thought. If we made good-looking shirts and they were not expensive, our audience would buy them. If this was bad idea, listeners would simply not buy the shirts and we would find out soon enough. I was on my own with my idea.

Our station audience was mostly young men between the ages of 15 and 30. I calculated the average listener wardrobe was shorts, T-shirts, bathing suits and sandals. Honolulu is year round beach weather and every day was T-shirt day. If we could get listeners to wear 98Rock logo shirts and make them part of the wardrobe, it would be the same effect the license plate promotion had in Orlando. But for this to work, literally thousands and thousands of T-shirts would have to be sold.

I called Robert and told him what happened when we gave the wallets away. I ran my new idea by him. I said, "We have a good morning show working, our TV advertising is starting to get us attention and the music is sounding good. Now we have listeners that want something from the station with the logo. But we have no money to buy merchandise and give things away free. We'll have to find a way for retailers to buy and sell the clothes and merchandise it for us. We can't handle this promotion through the radio station; our staff is too small to take on any more work."

I said, selling T-shirts would be the answer to the visibility problem and back our TV advertising. We'll call retailers that sell our merchandise the "98Rock Shops" so they can have a promotion identity.

Robert liked the idea and said he wanted to manufacture the T-shirts and all the merchandising for the station. He said, "I have lots of retail and wholesale connections in the state," and he had other promotional ideas of his own. Robert became a part of our station marketing team.

I created a licensing program for retailers to sell the logo clothing line. We told the retailers they were responsible to let listeners know where they could buy the 98Rock merchandise. That way the station would generate new sales revenues through advertising and the retailers would get the store traffic. It was a great idea for everyone, or so I thought.

No Believers

I sent our sales teams out to sell this idea to advertisers and we drew a blank, no results. No one believed this idea would work. Retailers had no faith in the new radio station and could not understand why anyone would pay for a radio station logo T-shirt. I called Robert and told him the problem. Robert said he had a friend that was a buyer and merchandiser for a man's clothing store. The store was in a good location and looking for new ideas to get younger customers.

"They might listen to this idea," Robert said.

Kramer's Men's Wear was in the huge Ala Mona shopping center. Robert and I met with the owner and staff. We explained what 98Rock was and how it could help the image of the store. But Kramer was thinking, who would pay for a T-shirt with a radio station logo on it? Of course, his being in the clothing business, he knew more about selling clothes than people from the radio station!

But the others in this meeting were not so sure this was a bad idea. Some were seeing that the promotion might work. It could bring in store traffic and new customers. Robert and I were doing our best to sell our concept but Kramer would not commit to buying any advertising. He would not budge and I could see we might lose this opportunity.

It's Free, That's a Big Discount

"OK, It's free," I said. We must have this anchor store and location to sell other retailers, I thought. This will get everything started for the promotion.

"We'll give Kramer's the promotional advertising announcements on the air free and a six-month exclusive, but only for the mall and one location. You buy the 98Rock merchandise from Robert. If the clothing sales are strong and you want to continue, we can talk about licensing at that point."

The store agreed to give us about 80 square feet of space so we could build a sales booth; it would be just inside the front entrance. The radio commercials went on the air promoting, "The 98Rock Shop Is Coming to Kramer's."

We were running promotional commercials so heavy it sounded like Kramer's was on every commercial break and a partner in the radio station. But the announcements were creative, very funny and we felt this big push would help the station's image.

On Saturday, the day of the opening, I arrived at the mall early. It was 8:30 AM and no stores in the mall were open. But parking spaces as far as I could see were filled. I went to the back entrance of Kramer's and asked the staff how things were going and looked outside the front store windows. A huge crowd was waiting to get in the store and hundreds of listeners were waiting in lines winding around corners in the mall. We were speechless.

We had our answer; the plan was now in full gear. Word got out quickly and retailers were calling the station to find out how to get a 98Rock Shop. We were able to get 13 stores committed to buying the merchandise. T-shirts were selling so fast they became the number one single design T-shirt sold in the state and advertising dollars were flowing.

The radio stations ratings soared to number one FM station in Honolulu and achieved 9th rank Album Rock station in the country. Robert's book says,

> In 1981, our downsized company entered a joint venture with a local radio station and created what is to this day reportedly the most successful merchandising program in the history of radio. Together with the radio station, we created a merchandising brand named 98Rock. The star product was a black T-shirt with a splashed paint logo of red and white, screaming 98Rock FM Honolulu. In Honolulu, our 98Rock Shops had thousands of kids lining up to buy tens of thousands of T-Shirts and other accessories.
> **—Robert Kiyosaki**
> Rich Dad's, Before You Quit Your Job

The radio station got on its feet and Robert was able to get his manufacturing business moving ahead once again. It was a great success for everyone.

The stories of ZETA7 and 98Rock are "Acts of Commission, Not Omission." This means, above all, take action. You get zero credit for what you don't do. You must take the risks to get the rewards.

I have come to realize that the action taken is even better than the strategy you work so hard at. The visions, dreaming, thinking and planning are only the setup to making success a reality.

The successful people I know in my life all have one thing in common. They are doing what they enjoy and they are enjoying what they do. They have superior people skills and work hard to get along with others. Get ideas from successful people that have real life experience, don't be afraid to ask for help.

Steps to Success

- **People Resist Change**
- **Don't Take No For An Answer**
- **Big Rocks Are Hard To Move, Until They Until They Start to Roll Down Hill**
- **What Counts: Acts Of Commission, Not Omission**

Chapter 11

Business 101- Evolution

Now here, you see, it takes all the running you can do to keep in the same place. If you want to get somewhere else, you must run at least twice as fast as that.

—**Lewis Carroll**
Through the Looking Glass

It's risky business predicting the future. Over time it's proven mass thinking and guru predicting is no better than most individuals can do. The founder of Digital Equipment Corporation in 1977 told us, "There is no reason anyone would want a computer in their home." The British Parliamentary Committee in 1878 proclaimed Edison's light bulb, "Unworthy of the attention of practical or scientific men."

Looking ahead, it helps to know where you have been. History gives perspective and insight. Experience teaches us to watch what *is* taking place and read between the lines of news reporting and editorial columns. It's also a good idea to get information from more than one source. As events unfold, be willing to evaluate and think for yourself. No one can predict the future, your guess may be as good as anyone's. As we move forward, technology, communication and global competition has put us on a fast track, and the *rate* of change has also accelerated. As knowledge and information grows, it's instantly available everywhere. More and more people across the planet work on innovations to make our lives better and more productive.

"Good Times"

The 50s through the late 70s were the "good times." The average worker was enjoying a secure job and good benefits. Productivity gains were modest and relatively few jobs were eliminated due to advances in technology. By the mid 70s, semiconductors, small computers and software developments were on the move. However, the mass markets considered personal computers high tech toys for hobbyist and the rich. The software at that time made computers difficult to use, hard to learn and not productive for many simple tasks.

In the 80s, computer programmers worked to convert the programming system of archaic software code into a new kind of software that ran graphics, pictures, sound and video. These advances made computers powerful tools that anyone could master. Business saw the benefits of this new technology and personal computers were becoming commonplace in offices and manufacturing everywhere.

However, the advances in technology seemed like baby steps compared to the gigantic leap about to come.

Warp Speed Communications

The Internet had been around for years used by researchers and the government but unavailable to the masses. A breakthrough in technology and software communications made the Internet available to virtually everyone with a phone modem and a computer.

At first, many did not grasp the concept of a world-wide broadcasting information dissemination medium that collectively sent, received and posted information. The internet had no regard to geographic location and was so on the edge, people simply didn't grasp the concept. *At first!*

But once word got around, it spread like wildfire. People began to understand what this "Internet thing" was. The demand to get online exploded and millions of people, organizations and companies signed up for AOL, Prodigy, and CompuServe. In no time at all, it was hard doing business without the internet.

Experts improved connection speeds to make the service even more usable. Pictures, sound, video, news, files, instant messages and email could be sent from anywhere around the planet at light speed. Email had became as important as mail and many were spending more time on computers than watching television.

As millions of web pages were getting posted to the Internet, new services and companies started. Remote countries and places were connected and virtually all known knowledge became available to anyone that knew how to search for it. This was transforming business and markets. Companies that relied on old business models and outdated technology found themselves commoditized or forced out of business. The Internet had proven to be a structural change. The status quo for business and the workplace was over. Fast-forward was now normal.

Money Goes Fast

"Money goes where it's needed and stays where it's wanted," says an old investors proverb. Technology speeds things up and moves money around even faster. Computers and software boost productivity for everyone. Technology allows money to follow emerging markets easier and take advantage of opportunities.

However, changes are not democratic or equal. As global competition finds efficiency, it creates new opportunities but at the same time devastating less efficient markets and jobs. The Internet, the big engine behind change, is a worldwide sledgehammer that drives down the cost of business.

Low Prices Come at High Costs

Getting more for less may be a paradox. Lifestyles improve with better products brought to the marketplace at lower costs. But salaries may lag as productivity increases. Computers and software help companies but they may also be competitive to jobs. Working 24/7, computers don't demand higher wages or cost of living increases. Experts are undecided if it's technology or globalization keeping wages in check. But it seems to matter little as the free global marketplace dictates wages. We do not compete with ourselves, we compete with the world.

Emerging economies have lower infrastructure and costs to deal with. They use lower wages as a competitive advantage to gain trade and opportunity. This keeps a temporary lid on salaries of developed countries. China, India, and Asia as well as the Hungarians, Czechs and Russians are competing for wealth and position in the new world order. It's a rolling cycle. As markets are developing, companies move to take advantage of lower costs. Developing countries bring millions of new people to the workforce. Many of the new workers have competitive skills and higher education.

Companies are created to make a profit and return the investment to it's stockholders and investors. It's the obligation of business to grow and be as profitable as markets and the economy allows. All jobs are affected when society or technology changes, *but not all jobs are affected equally.* New technologies allow companies to be more competitive and one way is to outsource telecommuting, software, engineering, and service jobs for efficiency and costs. As long as government and society allows it, companies will follow cheaper labor and tax advantaged markets to lower their costs, improve productivity and generate more profits.

Mass market discounters like Costco and Wal-Mart pass along the savings to consumers in the form of lower prices. Politicians complain of lost jobs and lower salaries as waves of super discount stores roll across America selling many products from other countries. Consumers come to big discount stores in droves for the endless variety of cost saving products.

Globalization creates winners and losers and that will be hard to control. The last time the United States tried to stop global trade and help workers was during the 1930s. The Great Depression was made worse by government efforts to protect people. Curtailing free trade produced devastating layoffs.

As worldwide productivity and innovation create more and better products at lower costs, business and workers will need to adjust and learn new skills to perform their jobs.

Churning the Economy

Early in 2005, Alan Greenspan, Chairman of the Board of Governors of the Federal Reserve and one of the most influential economist of all time appeared before Congress. He pointed out what happened in America as it opened up its system of world trading:

"A very substantial amount of America's prosperity is a consequence of an opening up of the world trading system over the last 50 years. Everybody has benefited from the increasing globalization.

I do not deny that as you get globalization, and the churning of the economy, there are winners and losers. But the number of winners is far in excess of the number of losers, and the resources that are created in the process can help take care of those on the wrong side of the trade-off.

A very major portion of our current standard of living rests on our position in the global markets. If we start to retreat from that, we will find we are very significantly impaired with respect to living standards.

Competition is not something anybody likes. But the more we liberalize trade, and the more we expand it, the higher our standards of living. We might prefer to be quiescent and not engage in so much competition, and we can do that, but there's a cost, and the cost is very significant."

Consumer spending is one of the largest parts of the U.S. economy. For growth and prosperity to continue, it is important to keep consumers healthy. But with increased global competition, many companies may not be able to raise prices or gain market share even as consumption increases. Workers everywhere are affected as salaries and prosperity are tied together. The Global economy is not static and moves as markets and demand changes.

The Storm was Brewing

The roaring stock markets of the 90s topped out early in 2000. Business started to slow. This appeared to be part of the normal business cycle of ups and downs. While the economic slow down was continuing we experienced the tragic event on September 11, 2001. Everyone focused on terrorism and those problems masked the brewing business storm. As the economy was slowing, *productivity was hitting all time highs.*

The Fed lowered interest rates to levels not seen in generations in an effort to help the economy get back on its feet. This created a spectacular building and housing boom that boosted the economy. Mortgage rates dove and millions refinanced their houses to get lower mortgage payments and take out tax-free cash from their home equity. Real estate became a piggy bank for homeowners and lifestyles improved for millions. However, *salaries and income barely budged during this period as the economy recovered.*

The lag time of technological advances during the 1970s through the 1990s had caught up. Thanks to technology, software and the Internet, companies were able to increase profits with fewer workers. The rich got richer and the middle class continued to shrink.

American manufacturing continues to lose jobs to foreign countries, it's part of a long-term trend. Many of the technologies and expertise the United States created and developed drives global manufacturing.

Forward Thinking

The United States economy has been built on freedom of trade, free enterprise, limited government interference, ingenuity, creativity and a tax system that favors business and entrepreneurs. But it has not been the best at being a low cost provider. Fast track global competition is catching up and companies won't have a safe and easy road to follow.

As world wide markets develop, the United States must remain on the leading edge of innovation. If you get there first, the competition is behind you. And if you get a big enough lead, catching you won't be easy. America must win on its brains and ingenuity.

Imagination is more important than knowledge.
—Albert Einstein

Entrepreneurs Get New Respect

Entrepreneurs by nature, are on the edge of creativity, innovation and driven by opportunity and profits. They are agnostic in their thinking and their challenge is to see new ways of doing things that others do not. They are not motivated by old ways of thinking and use that to their advantage.

Their management and leadership style is to keep people focused on success and rely on ideas and brainpower as a resource and less on structure. Entrepreneurs are as likely to disrupt a going business as much to as create new ones to find opportunities.

Global competitors are relentless working at creating new ideas they can bring to market. They also look for weakness in current products, systems and try to find better ways of doing things. No business or product is safe if it is not advanced to evolving competitive levels.

Entrepreneurs are also real business leaders that get a bad rap. As Rodney Dangerfield said, "They don't get no respect." For years, it was said entrepreneurs could start a business but could not manage one successfully. Now I realize this thinking was years of bureaucratic hierarchal managers protecting their egos and careers. Only a certain kind of training and those knowledgeable in planning and controlling can do the managing job. Entrepreneurs are not capable managers and the U.S. profitability of the 50s through the 70s proved that point. So they said.

But many companies during the 50s through the 70s did not face world-class competition, creativity, innovation and lower costs. Many of the successful companies were *only* successful because of *the lack of global competition.*

Bill Gates of Microsoft, Michael Dell of Dell Computers, Richard Branson of Virgin Airlines are all entrepreneurs and innovators. They didn't finish colleges and follow the established hierarchical management rules as they created new companies.

These new companies allowed many to get in the equity game. The companies started as small business with entrepreneurial spirit. And now these companies are considered the best-managed, innovative and creative.

Old paradigms may keep established businesses from maximizing opportunities when markets change. It's important for businesses to react to competition and threats with new ideas and thinking. Simply protecting resources and established ways of doing business may not create opportunities as the world changes. In some cases, doing the same old thing will put them out of business.

To the Future: Innovation & Creativity

Companies that work on improving relationships with employees will be best able to deal with change. For years, business focused on guarding against domestic competitors and managing a hierarchal style. But with new challenges, companies must adjust to new thinking.

Talented workers will be in high demand. A company not investing in its people as the prized resource is looking for trouble. It takes energized, motivated and talented people to keep a company on the leading edge and competitive.

Companies with good environments attract the best talent. Good environments create better places for people to work. Motivated people working on innovation and creativity is the future. Success will be the knowledge we gain and what we do with it. Companies and workers alike will evolve to a new way of doing business and more than ever, will be dependent on each other for success.

A new emphasis will be on creativity and innovation and a new style of management will lead an enlightened work force.

The art of campaign teaches us to rely not on the likelihood of the enemy's not coming, but on our own readiness to receive him; not on the chance of his not attacking, but rather on the fact that we have made our position unassailable.

—Sun Tzu

Thank you for taking the time to read my book. I wish you the best in your efforts and happiness in your life.

To your freedom, independence and success,

Brian J. Bieler

Steps to Success

- **Don't Wait For Change *To Happen To You***
- **"It Worked Before," Has Little Relevance In Global Competition**
- **Productivity Has Limits, Creativity And Innovation Has No Bounds**
- **"Do, Or Do Not. There Is No Try" — Yoda, Jedi Master, *Star Wars***

A Final Thought

Living with Dyslexia

I couldn't read. I just scraped by. My solution back then was to read classic comic books because I could figure them out from the context of the pictures. Now I listen to books on tape.

—Charles Schwab
Founder Charles Schwab stock brokerage

It was 1984, we were living Potomac, Maryland just outside of Washington DC. My wife Ann came in the bathroom as I am shaving and said, "Look at this article in USA Today. It is about dyslexia. Drew has all the symptoms in the article." I said, what is dyslexia? This was the first time I had ever heard of it.

Drew was in 5th grade and struggling. His teachers never mentioned why he was having a problem. They said he was a slow learner and school was difficult for him. But Drew was bright and normal in every respect, except he hated to read. I thought he was going to be a late bloomer as I was.

Ann took Drew to our pediatrician. The doctor said Drew was in excellent health. "But if he is having problems in school, have him tested." Ann brought Drew to a clinic in Bethesda specializing in learning disorders and they put him through a week of testing. I felt bad for Drew; his spring vacation spent in a testing booth.

After a battery of tests we knew why Drew was struggling in school, he was dyslexic. We were astounded his teachers never mentioned dyslexia. We discovered that teachers at that time were in the dark as much as we were.

The clinic described dyslexia as a learning disorder and said it had nothing to do with intelligence. They said the word dyslexia comes from the Greek, meaning "difficulty with words or language." Drew suffered in reading but he was creative and perceptive. Like blind people develop keen hearing, dyslexics do the same and compensate for their weakness using other skills. Dyslexia can be mild or severe and effects people differently.

For some people, the genius did not occur in spite of dyslexia, but because of it. This is not a disease, it will never change and you cannot fix it. We could teach Drew what to look for and help him compensate for his reading problems.

"What can we do as parents?" I asked.

They said the most important thing to do is reinforce his confidence. School has been a bad experience; Drew knows his grades have been poor. He needs to understand he is no dummy, and even gifted in areas. And, he will do much better in school if his tests are not timed.

"Is this hereditary?" I asked.

"Individuals can inherit this condition from a parent," was the answer.

I was dyslectic; the doctors were describing my symptoms. I felt like I was hit on the head with a frying pan. So this was why I was so awful in school! I could only pass grades going to summer school. I had a straight D+ or C- average except for gym, metal shop and history. I was a slow reader and had to re-read everything to comprehend what I had read.

I was in third grade and held after class because I couldn't understand the difference between their and there. I mixed up 3 and E, I never did figure out how to diagram a sentence. I did have a huge comic collection and could leaf through pages like a racecar, and had a virtual photographic memory of what I had collected. I could remember the torque, horsepower and displacement for every car engine made between 1955 and 1960. Mind twisting puzzles were easy for me to figure out yet I have a poor memory for people's names.

Luckily, while my grades suffered terribly in high school, I could hang out with my older brother and his college friends. They included me in everything and I was treated as an equal. The University of Miami gave me an aptitude test and told me I had set a curve for raw mechanical aptitude, the highest score they had recorded to date. However, my reading skills were poor and I would struggle in college with most of the required courses.

My perception skills were strong and I could read people well. I was intuitive. I loved computers and could understand them better than books. I learned how to take my creative and visual skills and use them to advantage in business. I found spreadsheets and financials easy to read by turning numbers into charts and graphs. I learned how to create radio ratings charts on accounting paper. In 1980, on an Apple II I discovered how to interpret radio programming advantages and deficiencies hidden in the sea of numbers with graphs. When I heard that Apple had created a new Macintosh computer that could do graphics, I waited in line for two hours to buy one.

I compensated for my dyslexia by overcompensating with visual and creative skills. In writing this book, I am lucky my wife and daughter are excellent readers. They helped me with drafts and editing as every page I wrote came back filled with red corrections. Ann would say, "It's a great read, but you are so awful with spelling and grammar. Thank God you have me to pick up after you," she said with a smile.

Yes, I thought, we laugh at my dyslexia.

Drew, with help, did not have to suffer in school as I did. He went from Ds and Fs to graduating college with a degree in communications. He overcomes things as I do by turning things around; he thinks creatively to work out problems.

The best thing we did for Drew was to give him confidence. We convinced him he was a smart kid and it did wonders. In spite of my family financial problems when I was young, my parents always supported me and gave me confidence.

They estimate that 40 to 60 million people in the U.S. have some form of dyslexia. Learn about it and make it a gift if possible. Get help for yourself and get help for your kids in school. Don't dwell on the problem it creates; make it something you can live with, find what you can excel at. It's not debilitating once you figure out how to deal with it. It's just a different way of thinking and it has unique advantages.

I ran companies and competed with bright people in a competitive business for years. Dyslexia never held me back and it helped my creativity. Many times, I was able to solve problems because I could see things from a unique perspective. Dyslexia has little to do with intelligence or competence; it's a learning disorder.

You may be able to improve your life if you master the skills I have outlined in this book. Both people skills and interpersonal skills are the secret assets of the successful. It is a way of thinking and seeing things. These skills have little to do with reading or math and are a natural for dyslexics to master.

The outlook on life is critical. With even a touch of dyslexia, a positive attitude becomes even more important.

Good luck and stay upbeat about yourself. Attitude determines altitude.

Some Famous Dyslexics:

Robin Williams, Billy Bob Thornton, Tommy Hilfinger, Jay Leno, Magic Johnson, Alexander Graham Bell, Tom Cruise, Leonardo da Vinci, Cher, Agatha Christie, Winston Churchill, Thomas Edison, Albert Einstein, Fannie Flagg, Danny Glover, Whoopi Goldberg, Bruce Jenner, Nelson Rockefeller, George Washington, Woodrow Wilson, Henry Winkler, Andy Warhol, Agatha Christie, General George Patton,

About the Author

Brian J. Bieler

Brian J. Bieler has more than thirty years of business, managing and sales experience. He began his career selling copy paper and by the age of twenty-four was a sales supervisor in midtown Manhattan. Brian then went into the advertising business at Women's Wear Daily and Mademoiselle Magazine in New York City. Later he joined Sudbrink Broadcasting, a leading-edge radio group specializing in buying and improving underperforming companies.

Brian became an accomplished executive in local, regional and national broadcasting. He was Vice President and General Manager of ten major market radio stations from coast to coast and President of the Viacom Radio Group in New York City. He knows how to operate a business from start-up to planning strategies, marketing, and sales.

"People everywhere have similar wants and needs. Different environments change their behavior and outlook. I saw the best performance in companies when people were encouraged to be innovative, creative, and able to work in entrepreneurial situations. Letting people take ownership of what they do is smart business, it lets them bring out the best in themselves," says Brian.

Much of Brian's success is due to his learning communication skills, keeping people motivated and being sure the entrepreneurial spirit thrives.

Brian is an author, entrepreneur, and corporate leader.

Quick Order Form

Telephone Orders: 800-980-5099

Email Book Orders or contact: www.powerfuteps.com

Postal Orders:
    Powerful Steps
    7000 North 16th Street, Suite 120 #489
    Phoenix, AZ, 85020

Please send (number of copies_____) Powerful Steps to:

Name (please print):_____

Address:_____

City:_____State:_____Zip:_____

Country:_____

Telephone:_____

Email address:_____

$17.95 U.S. Dollars per book.

Sales Tax If Shipped To Arizona Residents: Please add 8.1%

U. S. Shipping and Handling add $4.00 per book and $2.00 for each additional book in same shipment.

International Shipping and handling add $8.00 per book and $5.00 for each additional book in same shipment.

Payment: Cheque:☐   Credit Card:☐

Visa☐   Master Card☐   AMEX☐   Discover☐

Card Number:_____

Name On Card:_____

Expiration Date On Card_____

Printed in the United States
70928LV00004BB/82